CALVINISM
in the
LAS VEGAS
AIRPORT

Also by Richard Mouw

The Smell of Sawdust

CALVINISM
in the
LAS VEGAS
AIRPORT

making
connections
in today's
world

RICHARD J. MOUW

GRAND RAPIDS, MICHIGAN 49530 USA

ZONDERVAN™

Calvinism in the Las Vegas Airport
Copyright © 2004 by Richard J. Mouw

Requests for information should be addressed to:
Zondervan, *Grand Rapids, Michigan 49530*

Library of Congress Cataloging-in-Publication Data
Mouw, Richard J.
   Calvinism in the Las Vegas airport : making connections in today's world / Richard J. Mouw.
      p. cm.
   Includes bibliographical references and index (p.   ).
   ISBN 0-310-23197-3 (hardcover)
1. Calvinism.   2. Reformed Church—Creeds—History and criticism.   3. Synod of Dort (1618–1619) Canones Synodi Dordrechtanae.   I. Title.
   BX9422.3.M68 2004
   230'.42—dc22

                                                       2004007231

This edition printed on acid-free paper.

Interior design by Tracey Moran

Printed in the United States of America

05 06 07 08 09 10 /❖ DC/ 10 9 8 7 6 5 4 3 2

For Peter and Willem

CONTENTS

ACKNOWLEDGMENTS

Even though I worked on this book in fits and starts over a sixteen-month period, I got off to a great beginning (always the hardest part for me) in a wonderful environment—a home in a beautiful wooded setting outside Princeton, New Jersey, where Phyllis and I spent a two-week study leave in July 2002. This was a gift of hospitality from Judy and Jim Bergman. I also received a second gift from Jim: when he found out what I was writing about, he shared with me his own wrestlings with some key Calvinist ideas. His probings on these matters were an important stimulus for me in my efforts to make my thoughts on these matters clearer.

I have learned so much from so many people over the years about the subjects discussed in these pages that I could not possibly give adequate credit to all who deserve it. But I do need to express special thanks to three people who were willing to give a careful reading to an earlier draft of this book.

My daughter-in-law, Christine Mouw, not only provided a number of incisive suggestions, but she also warned me against some stilted language by reminding me of a critical comment that one of her husband's undergraduate history students once wrote on a teacher evaluation: "Dude needs to tone down the vocab!"

Mark Edwards of Harvard Divinity School is a friend who does much to keep my Calvinism honest from his perspective as a Lutheran and a Luther scholar.

And my Fuller colleague John Thompson, who knows much more than I do about the history of Calvinist thought, helped me to clarify what I meant—or should have meant—at several key points.

I also received excellent guidance and encouragement along the way from Zondervan editor Paul Engle. My enjoyment of our conversations about this project was enhanced by memories of the times we discussed some of these same matters together as undergraduates many years ago at Houghton College.

All of these folks were so helpful, and I was so diligent in taking full advantage of their wise counsel, that any remaining errors or infelicities must simply be chalked up either to the mysteries of divine predestination or—more likely—to the subtle but very real continuing marks of my own depravity.

chapter 1

HARDCORE TULIP

I have been thinking about writing this book ever since I saw the film *Hardcore*. A movie with a title like that will not strike most folks as an obvious source of inspiration for some reflections on how to be a Calvinist in the twenty-first century, so I had better explain myself.

Hardcore was directed by Paul Schrader, who had graduated from Calvin College in Grand Rapids, Michigan, just before I arrived there in 1968 as a new faculty member. Even though Schrader had gone off to do graduate study in film at UCLA, he was still being talked about much on the Calvin campus—and the commentary expanded to legendary proportions during the next seventeen years I served on the faculty. Schrader's very public rebellion against his religious upbringing had already been in full swing during his undergraduate years, a pattern that had disappointed the college community. But for all of that, they monitored his successes with obvious interest, as he moved from doctoral work in film studies at UCLA into the Hollywood limelight as a screenwriter and director. You could even detect a kind of embarrassed pride in us Grand Rapids folks—and I include myself here—when some journalist would quote his comments about "the narrow-minded Dutch Calvinism" that had been such a formative influence in his youth.

We kept track of all of his movies—*Taxi Driver* and *American Gigolo* were two of his early successes—even though the content was quite racy for folks like us. But the one that created the biggest local buzz was *Hardcore*. Schrader filmed it in Grand Rapids, and that itself was enough to build the excitement. The film people borrowed a well-known Christian Reformed minister's robe for the church service scene, and we all knew where the house was in which they shot the family dinner event.

I don't recommend *Hardcore* for people seeking spiritual edification. But there is one scene in the film that I have regularly pondered in my own theological reflections. Jake Van Dorn, a pious Calvinist elder played by George C. Scott, is sitting in the Las Vegas airport with a thoroughly pagan young woman named Niki. Jake's teenage daughter has run away to California and gotten involved in the pornography business, and he has set out to find her. His initial efforts thus far have failed, but he has managed to enlist the help of Niki, a young prostitute who knows his daughter. They have just followed a lead in Las Vegas, but having discovered that the wayward daughter is no longer there, they are moving on in their search.

CONVERSATION IN THE LAS VEGAS AIRPORT

As they are sitting in the boarding area, waiting for their plane, Niki informs Jake that she considers him to have a very negative outlook on life, and it is obviously connected, she thinks, to his religious beliefs. "What kind of church do you belong to?" she asks. "It's a Dutch Reformed denomination," he responds, "—a group that believes in TULIP." The conversation continues:

> *Niki:* What the crap?
> *Jake:* It's an acronym. It comes from the Canons of Dordt. Every letter stands for a different belief, like—Are you sure you want to hear this?
> *Niki:* Yeah, yeah. Please go on. I'm a Venusian myself.

Jake: Well, **T** stands for "total depravity": all men through original sin are totally evil and incapable of good. All my works are as filthy rags in the sight of the Lord.

Niki: That's what the Venusians call negative moral attitudes.

Jake: Be that as it may, **U** stands for "unconditional election": God has chosen a certain number of people to be saved, the elect, and he's chosen them from the beginning of time. **L** is for "limited atonement": only a limited number of people will be atoned and go to heaven. **I** is for "irresistible grace": God's grace cannot be resisted or denied. And **P** is for the "perseverance of the saints": once you're in grace, you cannot fall from the numbers of the elect. That's it.

Niki: Before you can become saved, God already knows who you are?

Jake: Oh yes, he'd have to. That's predestination. I mean, if God is omniscient, if he already knows everything—and he wouldn't be God if he didn't—then he must have known, even before the creation of the world, the names of those who would be saved.

Niki: Well, then, it's all worked out, huh? It's fixed.

Jake: More or less.

Niki: I thought *I* was ****ed up.

Jake: Well, I admit it's a little confusing when you look at it from the outside. You have to try to look at it from the inside.

Let me say right off that I get the joke. Schrader is poking some fun at his tradition, and he learned his catechism lessons well. It is the obvious incongruity of the situation that makes it so funny: a puritanical Grand Rapids Dutchman solemnly summarizing the teachings of the seventeenth-century synod that met in the Dutch city of Dordrecht—often shortened to "Dordt"—to a theologically clueless, profane Valley girl.

HUMOROUS BUT DISTURBING

I see the humor—but I also find the scene very disturbing. It symbolizes a deep personal struggle for me. The beliefs that Jake describes are important to me. At the same time, though, I live as a twenty-first-century Calvinist in a world where Niki's way of viewing things is in the ascendancy. The struggle to connect the two ways of experiencing reality is a daily one for me. I believe that TULIP, properly understood, captures something very central to the gospel. And I want to bring that gospel to Niki and her kind. Because of that, Jake's conversation-ending observation that "You have to try to look at it from the inside" is not good enough for me. I want to invite people like Niki *into* that "inside."

Jake's way of responding to Niki exemplifies for me a typical pattern among Calvinists. We take seriously the apostle's mandate, "Always be prepared to give an answer to everyone who asks you to give the reason for the hope that you have" (1 Peter 3:15). And Jake surely fulfilled the literal requirement here: the young woman asked him what he believed, and he responded with a straightforward summary of Calvinist doctrine. But in what seems to me an all-too-typical Calvinist fashion, he did not acknowledge the rest of what the apostle requires. The verse in question continues, "But do this with gentleness and respect."

While I sincerely subscribe to the TULIP doctrines, I have to admit that, when stated bluntly, they have a harsh feel about them. To articulate them "with gentleness and respect" takes some effort. Indeed, I am not convinced that summarizing the TULIP teachings is really the best approach to take in a situation like the one depicted in *Hardcore*. I think it would have been more effective simply to turn the young woman's question back to her, encouraging her to talk about her own spiritual interests. What about those "Venusian" convictions she referred to in her own way of viewing things? What, if any, are the deeper hopes and fears that motivate her in dealing with the basic issues of life? And in probing these matters, it would be important to stay on the lookout for an opportunity to point her to the heaven-sent Savior who went to the cross so that messed-up lives could be put back together again.

But, again, I believe that TULIP captures some very important elements of the story of salvation's plan. And I would hope that if she were to accept Jesus as her Savior, Niki would eventually come to understand the basic issues at stake in the TULIP doctrines. But I would want to lead her in that direction "with gentleness and respect."

I must also say up front that it isn't just in our conversations with unbelievers that I find many Calvinists lacking in gentleness and respect. I even find these qualities missing in Calvinists' interactions with other *Christians.* Indeed, Calvinists are often not very gentle and respectful when debating fine points of doctrine with fellow *Calvinists.*

I worry a lot about these Calvinist habits of mind and heart. What does Calvinism have to say to our present world? How can I best *be* a Calvinist in the twenty-first century? How do I as a TULIP-lover speak gently and respectfully to non-Christians about what I believe? How do I articulate my Calvinist convictions gently and respectfully to fellow Christians who see things quite differently than I do? What do the Canons of Dordt mean for people who hang around in the Las Vegas airport?

These are the questions that have led me to write this book. I will be wrestling with them in the pages that follow.

chapter 2

FOR DISTINCTION'S SAKE

f you need a systematic exposition of Calvinist thought, you are not going to find it here. There is plenty of that to be found elsewhere. John Calvin's own *Institutes of the Christian Religion* is clearly the best place to go for the basics,[1] but other sorts of writings also do a good job—large books of Calvinist systematic theology[2] and shorter works devoted to explaining and defending some part of Calvinist teaching, for example. You can even take your pick from many introductory explanations of the TULIP doctrines in particular. Just before I wrote these sentences I did a Google search for "five points of Calvinism," which turned up over three thousand items, many of them expositions you can read on the Web.

My main focus here is not on *what* Calvinists believe. To be sure, I will actually get into some Calvinist specifics here and there. But I will not feel obliged to touch on everything that is important in the Calvinist perspective, taking the standard formulations for granted. I am more interested here in questions about Calvinist character and mood. I want to focus here on how to *be* a Calvinist in the twenty-first century. How can a person today connect the distinctive beliefs associated with Calvinism to a world very different from the one inhabited by earlier generations of Calvinists? This is a book for people who want to see how it is possible to draw on the strengths of Calvinism as they make their way through the complexities of contemporary life.

I have run across many people who have what I am convinced is a distorted view of Calvinism. I have met some folks, for example, who think that Calvinists are essentially very nasty people who have a strange understanding of what the Christian religion is all about. And, of course, I have met many people who call themselves Calvinists who actually *are* very nasty people who have a strange understanding of what the Christian religion is all about.

And then there are people like me. We are attracted to Calvinism, but we regret the fact that there are so many people who have such a distorted view of Calvinist thought and life. In these pages I am mainly interested in giving some help to those folks who would like to set the record straight. But in attempting to provide counsel for them, I hope, too, that I might actually change the outlook of some of the people who perpetuate the misunderstandings.

WHY USE THE LABEL *CALVINIST?*

When I mentioned to a friend that I was planning to write a book about being a Calvinist, he urged me to use a different label. "You'd be better off talking about being *Reformed,*" he said. "It gives the feel of something that is a little broader, and frankly it has a nicer feel than *Calvinist.*"

I appreciated the point he was making, but I decided not to take his advice. The Calvinist label is an important one for me. It was for Jonathan Edwards as well, and I have found his thoughts on the subject helpful. The great Puritan theologian was well aware of the negative associations of the Calvinist label, but he chose to embrace the term anyway. At the beginning of his great work titled *Freedom of the Will,* he wrote: "However the term *Calvinist* is, in these days, amongst most, a term of greater reproach than the term *Arminian;* yet I should not take it at all amiss, to be called a *Calvinist,* for distinction's sake."[3]

Edwards is not only right about *Calvinist* in particular; he is also making a good point about labels in general. Labels are helpful only if they make legitimate distinctions. They serve us well when they are informative, when they tell us something important about the person who chooses to use a specific label.

Like Edwards, I find it helpful to call myself a Calvinist "for distinction's sake." It says something important about what I believe, something not quite captured by any other label. And so, even given the bad connotations the label has, I willingly claim it for my own.

A HIERARCHY OF LABELS

I once read a nice explanation given by Lutheran scholar Martin Marty about the various labels he applies to himself. I know I read it several decades ago, because Marty was still a Missouri Synod Lutheran at the time. He was reporting his answer to someone who had asked him why he stayed in that denomination.

This is what I remember him saying: He is first and foremost a human being, but he finds being a Christian the best way for him to be a human being. And he finds being Protestant the best way for him to be a Christian. And he finds being Lutheran the best way for him to be a Protestant. And he finds—or at least he did so at the time—being Missouri Synod the best way for him to be a Lutheran. On this last point Marty added that, because he was raised as a Missouri Synod Lutheran, he knew all of its jokes, and he would hate to have to learn how to laugh at some other denomination's humor.

This may strike some people as a bit too droll. But there are two elements in Marty's explanation that I especially like. One is his emphasis on the role of very personal considerations in the way we connect ourselves to this or that Christian tradition. By highlighting the "for him" factor, Martin Marty is allowing for the way in which the facts of our individual biographies shape our allegiances. I don't take an "anything goes" approach to the business of forming theological loyalties, but I do recognize that our choices have something to do with what we see as "best" *for us,* given our individual spiritual needs and interests.

The other thing I like is the way Marty pushes all the other choices back to our basic humanness. In the final analysis, our allegiances have to be evaluated with reference to what kinds of human beings they help us to be. The philosopher Jean-Paul Sartre argued that, since there is no God, every important decision we make is an act of creation; implicit in all those choices, he said, was an image of humanness we are attempting to fashion. While I don't accept his notion of radical creative freedom, I do accept a Christian counterpart to his claim: God created us to glorify him in all we do, and our basic choices either honor or dishonor God's creating purposes. When I decide to call myself a Calvinist, then—and if I am serious in my declaration—I am implying that this is a very good way to be a human being who is created in the divine image. And in setting forth the merits of Calvinism, I am obliged to show how this way of being a Christian promotes human flourishing.

With Martin Marty's explanation in mind, here is how I explain my own set of steps. First and foremost, I am a human being. But I find being a Christian to be the best way for me to be a human being. And I find being Protestant the best way for me to be a Christian. And I find being Reformed the best way for me to be Protestant. And I find being a Calvinist to be the best way of being Reformed.

People who have read other things I've written may wonder where *evangelical* fits into all of this. That label is important to me too— indeed I have written a whole book explaining why being an evangelical is a key feature of my spiritual journey.[4] I'll not repeat here my reasons for liking this label, except to say that for me Calvinism and evangelicalism go nicely together.

Others might be puzzled about my insisting that Calvinism is *a* way of being Reformed, thus suggesting that there is a gap between the two identities. I don't want to make too big a deal about the distinction, except that I do occasionally come across theologians who want to be identified as Reformed but who do not particularly like the Calvinist label. When I have tried to get clear about why they object to being called Calvinists, I find that the things they do not like about Calvinism are often things that I *do* like. For example, they often want to downplay the TULIP doctrines in favor of some of the other theological themes introduced by John Calvin at the time of the Reformation. I usually like those other themes too, but I like to stick with the "Calvinist" label to signal that I see those other themes as built on the foundation of the TULIP teachings. And, of course, describing myself as a Calvinist also allows me to distance my views from those more liberal thinkers who like to use a term like "Reformed" as a slogan calling for a church that is constantly testing out new—and often rather strange—doctrines.

To put it another way, I embrace the Calvinist label to signal the fact that in general I find earlier Reformed thinkers more helpful than later ones. I subscribe sincerely and wholeheartedly to the Reformation-era confessions, particularly the three documents that have long defined doctrinal orthodoxy in the Dutch Reformed tradition: the Heidelberg Catechism, the Belgic Confession, and the Canons of Dordt.[5]

When I say I subscribe to these documents, I don't mean I'm prepared to defend them line by line. When I served on the faculty of Calvin College, each of us who taught there was required, as are all ordained officeholders in the sponsoring denomination, to give our written assent to the three Dutch Reformed confessional documents. Once when I was being tested for theological orthodoxy, my examiner asked me to explain the sense in which I claimed to agree with the content of the Canons of Dordt. I responded that as I read the Canons I'm not always sure why or how the Dordrecht gathering decided to say exactly what they did—but it isn't as though I would want to attempt a rewrite!

These documents speak to me from another time in history—but they do speak to me convincingly in what they basically teach. They serve as crucial reference points for me in my attempts to stay within the boundaries of Calvinist orthodoxy. And when I say that they are reference points, I mean that I really do refer to them frequently. I consider it an important part of my Calvinist discipline to study the confessional documents of the past on a regular basis.

My only serious misgivings about these documents have to do with the way they regularly portray opposing positions. Some of my good Christian friends hold to these positions, and while I like to argue with them about these important matters, I don't like the harsh language used by my Calvinist ancestors. So I read these older documents with a tendency to filter out the rhetorical excess.

HOW I BECAME A CALVINIST

I never made a record of the day and the hour I became a convinced Calvinist, but I do remember clearly how it happened. I was a freshman in college, and I had been regularly attending a local Christian Reformed church where the preaching was heavily doctrinal. The pastor was a very scholarly type, and he printed rather detailed outlines of his sermons in the Sunday bulletins. During the weeks I had been attending his preaching services, he was expounding the teachings of the Canons adopted by the Synod of Dordrecht (1618–19).

His preaching was quite a change of pace for me, and I was enjoying it. I had been raised in a fairly anti-intellectual sort of evangelicalism, and the idea that listening to sermons could be an intellectual exercise had never occurred to me before. But I was especially taken with the actual content of what he was preaching. The Calvinism of the Synod of Dordt struck me as a very compelling system of thought. The basic premise was about an all-powerful God who rescues sinners from their otherwise hopeless condition by sovereign grace. Heady stuff!

The very headiness of it also nagged at me, however. The whole thing seemed to foster a rather somber tone in the congregation's patterns of worship. The preaching was solid, but it lacked evangelical passion. Nor did the passion show up in any other part of the worship gathering. I decided I needed to supplement what I was getting at this church with a little bit of the spiritual fervor that had been so much a part of my upbringing. So on Sunday afternoons I made a point of reading one of the sermons of Charles Spurgeon, the great British Baptist preacher of the nineteenth century.

My parents had started giving me a few volumes at a time of Charles Spurgeon's sermons when I was still in high school. (Eventually I owned a full set of twenty volumes.) Their motives for doing so were transparent. One way to encourage a son to follow in his preacher-father's footsteps was to be sure he had plenty of sermon books on his bookshelves! I'm not sure that either of my parents were intimately familiar with Spurgeon's actual theology. But in our part of the evangelical world, Spurgeon was regularly described as "the prince of preachers," so that was probably enough for them to want me to have access to his wisdom. And I did actually start reading Spurgeon during these early months as a college student.

On this particular Sunday the Christian Reformed preacher had made a strong case for the doctrine of election. I had attended the service with a friend, and I remember telling him as we walked back to the campus that I was almost persuaded by the exposition we had just heard. He had been raised in those theological environs and found it puzzling that I would have any resistance at all. It did not help me when he rehearsed the arguments, because my reluctance had nothing to do with the logic of the case. I worried that this was not the kind of thing one could get *excited* about. Could someone preach this stuff with spiritual fervor?

That afternoon I opened a volume of my Spurgeon collection and glanced at the table of contents to see if any of the topics caught my attention. Much to my surprise I saw a sermon with a one-word title: "Election." I read through the sermon, and by the time I was finished

I knew that this was my kind of theology. The Christian Reformed sermon on election I had heard earlier had spoken powerfully to my mind. And now Spurgeon showed me that the same topic could move me in the deep places of my soul.

I reread Spurgeon's sermon recently in preparation for writing about it here, and I still experience its power.[6] It is no longer my favorite Spurgeon piece on the subject—I later discovered his wonderful essay "A Defense of Calvinism," which I'll be referring to as I move along in this discussion.[7] But the sermon I read as a college student still stands out for me as a model for combining some of the most basic things I cherish in my efforts to live an integrated Christian life: theological clarity, a sense of awe in the presence of divine sovereignty, a deep desire for holy living, and evangelistic fervor.

I had no inkling in those early days as a college student of the complex challenges I would face in the coming years. I would soon go through periods of serious doubt about basic issues of faith. And during the radical 1960s, as a graduate student on secular university campuses, I could not avoid struggling with questions of justice and peace. But at every point, I eventually found that Calvinism provided me with resources to deal with these challenges. My journey, then, has been one of continually discovering new riches in the Calvinist tradition.

But I also know that I could not have discovered the riches without first of all accepting the basics. So I will offer some thoughts now about what lies at the heart of the Calvinist perspective.

chapter 3

MERE CALVINISM

W hat is Calvinism all about, really? What does it come down to, underneath all the theological formulations that people set forth to defend it?

I'm going to offer my account of "mere" Calvinism here. But I do so in full awareness that this is a risky exercise. I have always thought that C. S. Lewis did a fine job setting forth the basics of the Christian faith in his book *Mere Christianity*. But every once in a while I come across someone who feels strongly that Lewis never really succeeded in getting the "mereness" right, that he actually stacked the deck in favor of a certain kind of Christianity and created a bias against other versions. Even so, I'm glad he made the effort. It helps to have some rough idea of the difference between the "mere" and the "more" in our understanding of Christianity. And the same holds for Calvinism. I feel strongly about the "more" in my understanding of the riches of Calvinist thought, and I'll bring quite a bit of attention to that as I move along. But first I want to make it clear how I understand the "mere."

WHAT TULIP EXPRESSES

It is interesting to start reading the Canons of Dordt with the question in mind of how far a non-Calvinist would get into the document before beginning to experience theological discomfort. My estimate is that it takes about a page of single-space text—a little over 350 words. This gets you through the first five articles, each of them a paragraph in length, of the First Head of Doctrine. The first article tells us that we are all sinners and worthy of God's righteous judgment. The second describes the love of God by paraphrasing John 3:16. The third emphasizes the importance of the preaching of the gospel. The fourth points to the two very different human responses to the gospel: refusal and acceptance. And the fifth states clearly that the responsibility for unbelief resides in the human sinner, while salvation is a free gift to those who believe.

So far so good, as I read it—recognizing, of course, that some people might want to nuance the statements differently along the way. But then the controversial topics emerge, as the sixth article insists that whether or not a person receives the gift of faith "stems from [God's] eternal decision," and the seventh article offers a detailed formulation of divine election. And from there on things get more and more Calvinistically complex, with an additional twenty-two pages of theological explanation. No wonder ordinary Calvinists developed the TULIP acronym to keep the basic picture in mind!

T = total depravity
U = unconditional election
L = limited atonement
I = irresistible grace
P = perseverance of the saints

Here is how I see the heart of the matter. Where the Calvinist departs from other theological systems is in the insistence on placing a central emphasis on *the sovereignty of God.* The TULIP doctrines focus on *soteriology*—the theology of salvation. They provide a complicated answer to this basic question: How does a human being get right with God? And the fundamental answer, as spelled out in TULIP, is that it is all God's doing. The *T* offers a picture of the human condition as a helpless one. We have gotten ourselves into a mess—"In Adam's fall we sinned all," as the old slogan goes—and we are totally incapable of getting ourselves out of it by our own efforts. If we are to be delivered from our desperate condition, then it will have to be because God takes the initiative—thus the *U*. And God has indeed made the crucial move; he sent his Son into the world to atone for the sins of those whom— here is the *L*—God had beforehand chosen to eternal life. *I*: God draws his chosen ones irresistibly to himself. And—*P*—once they enter into genuine fellowship with him, God will never abandon them.

Again, at the heart of all of this is a strong conviction about divine sovereignty. Not that only Calvinists believe in a sovereign God. To make that claim would be to bear false witness against many Christians of other theological persuasions. But unlike the other traditions, Calvinism rigorously guards this emphasis on divine sovereignty by refusing to allow any other theological point to detract from it. This refusal comes through most obviously in dealing with issues of human responsibility. The Bible clearly teaches both that God is sovereign and that human beings are responsible for the basic choices they make. And Calvinism does acknowledge both. As I've already observed, just before getting into the specifically Calvinist teachings, the Canons of Dordt make a point of insisting that God holds people responsible for rejecting the gospel.

So, like every other theological system, Calvinism acknowledges human responsibility. But when Calvinists get around to attempting to explain the relationship between God's sovereignty and human freedom, we are so concerned to protect the former that we are willing to risk sounding like we are waffling on the latter rather than to imply in any way that God's power is limited. Our instincts here are the opposite of many other Christians, who would much rather be accused of denying God's full sovereignty than to give the impression that they are putting curbs on human freedom.

Spurgeon put this whole point rather nicely. "If anyone should ask me what I mean by a Calvinist," he wrote, "I should reply, 'He who says, *Salvation is of the Lord.*'" He goes on to acknowledge that other Christians will make this same affirmation. But Calvinists, Spurgeon argues, get very nervous when others find it necessary rather quickly to bring in "the addition of something to the work of the Redeemer."[8] Calvinists will have nothing of that. We want to draw special and sustained attention to God's sovereignty as that which alone makes our salvation possible.

THE *T:* OUR HUMAN CONDITION

The strong emphasis on divine sovereignty is closely related in Calvinism to its understanding of the human condition. Since the TULIP doctrines are, as I have already observed, soteriological in their focus—they are concerned with how a person can get saved—they highlight our depraved condition as fallen creatures. But there is a more basic theme at work here. Even if we were not fallen, we would be totally dependent on God's goodwill. Here again Spurgeon is helpful. Even if we think of God entering into a covenantal relationship with *unfallen* people, he observes, the human being "is so insignificant a creature that it must be an act of gracious condescension on the Lord's part." But that God would enter into a covenant with "so offensive a creature" as a *fallen* human being—this could only be "an act of pure, free, rich, sovereign grace."[9]

Needless to say, Calvinists have some favorite proof texts to make the case about human depravity. But Spurgeon captures another important basis for our position when he testifies that "I am bound to the doctrine of the depravity of the human heart, because I find myself depraved in heart, and have daily proofs that in my flesh there dwelleth no good thing."[10]

Now, obviously, this appeal to experience can also work in the other direction. In one of his very funny novels satirizing religion, the writer Peter De Vries, who (like Paul Schrader) enjoyed casting his

Calvinist upbringing in a humorous light, narrates a conversation (probably only partly fictionalized) about the TULIP doctrines that his lead character—a person who had departed from his Dutch Calvinist upbringing for a career as a crusading liberal minister—had in his youth with his pious father. Commenting on the *T,* the budding theological skeptic challenged his father along these lines: "Oh, come now, people aren't all that bad. Take you, for instance. You're a good sort. In fact, I think you're quite a nice guy."[11]

That kind of assessment also seems to be dictated by our experience. Most of us interact daily with people who strike us as pretty good sorts. Any Calvinist who steps out into the world expecting to encounter only mean-spirited, self-serving reprobates is bound to be caught up short on a regular basis.

Even the Reformed confessional documents are ambivalent on this subject. The Heidelberg Catechism offers the same kind of unqualified verdict that Spurgeon gives when he says that he receives "daily proofs that in my flesh there dwelleth no good thing": according to the Catechism we are incapable of "*any* good" apart from saving grace.[12] The Canons of Dordt, on the other hand, introduce an important modifier, stipulating that all human beings "are conceived in sin and are born children of wrath, unfit for any *saving* good"[13]—thus suggesting that the real point is that we cannot do the sorts of good things that can contribute to our salvation.

I take the Canons to be making the more precise theological point on this subject. This way of viewing the matter has led some Calvinist theologians to offer the helpful explanation that our depravity is *total*—both in the sense that we are totally incapable of doing anything that merits salvation and in the sense that sin affects us in all dimensions of our nature—but not *absolute,* as if every single thought, desire, and action of our sinful natures are completely corrupted. Good things are accomplished by human beings—by both the regenerate and the unregenerate.

Nothing here negates Spurgeon's important appeal to experience, though. Indeed, I find his description of the state of his soul *prior* to his salvation to be a fairly accurate depiction of my own *Christian* experience. He can still recall, Spurgeon says, "what a den of unclean beasts and birds my heart was, and how strong was my unrenewed will, how obstinate and rebellious against the sovereignty of the Divine rule."[14] Those images capture the way I still experience life on a daily basis. I have a lot of sympathy for the comment British novelist Evelyn Waugh is reported to have made when someone asked how, given that he was such a mean-spirited human being, he could call himself a Christian. The truth of the matter, he replied, is that if it weren't for his Christianity he would barely be human at all!

Many memories of misdeeds in my life regularly cause me to shudder in horror at what I am capable of doing. I often reflect sadly, for example, on something that happened when I was only seven years old. A friend and I walked to and from school together, and we took a shortcut that led us alongside railroad tracks. Trains carrying coal traveled that route, and on the ground in that area were lumps of coal that had fallen from the cars. On many mornings we saw a child younger than ourselves walking with a pail and collecting coal. We knew he was very poor. He had no father, and his mother would send him out for fuel for their coal stove. One day we hid in the bushes until his pail was full, and then we jumped out, threw him to the ground, and scattered the coal in every direction. He began to cry, and we went on our way laughing.

The image of that weeping boy on the ground is a vivid one for me. Sometimes I now cry when I think about it. I try to imagine what was going on in my heart when I performed that absolutely gratuitous bit of evil, and I cannot fathom it. I don't understand how the boy who at that time loved to sing "Jesus loves the little children, all the children of the world" could also take delight in that child's tears. The experience certainly helps me understand the biblical texts we Calvinists cite when defending the doctrine of total depravity. I know in a very personal way, for example, that "the heart is deceitful above all things, and desperately wicked" (Jeremiah 17:9 KJV). And when I recoil in horror as I read about, say, "Christian" Nazi soldiers who herded the Jews into the ovens at Auschwitz, I know that at some deep level I am capable of the same despicable acts.

When other Christians tell me they see no need to endorse the doctrine of total depravity, I don't know how to give them decisive arguments that will prove to them they are wrong. But I not only accept the doctrine as theologically sound; I *feel* its truth in the depths of my being.

THE *U:* DIVINE SELECTIVENESS

I was invited to speak to a Jewish audience as part of a series about the Ten Commandments. I opened my talk by identifying myself as a Calvinist and noting that my tradition has probably paid more attention to the Law given at Sinai than most other Christian traditions. After the session a Jewish couple came over to thank me for my presentation. They said they appreciated my remarks but were puzzled by my reference to Calvinism. "You seem like a nice person," the woman said. "That's not the image we have of Calvinists." Her husband quickly added, "Yes—like, don't Calvinists believe that God elects certain people and not others? That seems to me to be a horrible belief!"

It wasn't the right setting for an extended discussion, so I said something about how Calvinism is more complex than that, and I exchanged a few pleasantries with them before taking my leave. But in reflecting on the brief exchange, I was struck by the irony of religious Jews complaining about a system of thought that featured divine selectivity. The notion of election—admittedly of a more "corporate" sort than we find in Calvinism—is at the heart of Jewish belief. God began his relationship with the Israelites by singling out Abram, rather than any of his neighbors in Ur, as the person—and his descendants—to whom the Lord would promise blessings. Subsequently, God made it clear that he favored the children of Israel over the Egyptians—and later than that over the Canaanites, and still later over the Philistines, and so on.

What Calvinists refer to as election and irresistible grace are not mere intellectual abstractions. They capture very real experiences of divine selectivity in our lives. I once talked to a Christian scholar who told me a moving story about how he became a Christian. He had no religious upbringing, and well into his thirties he had no identifiable interest in spiritual matters. He and his wife were both university professors, and their Sunday morning ritual was to eat bagels and read the *New York Times*. One Sunday morning, as he was returning from his usual bakery-and-newsstand excursion, he passed an Episcopal church. He heard the sounds of congregational singing, and much to his surprise he felt compelled to enter the building and sit in the back pew. Soon after he sat down, the congregation read together the prescribed prayer for confessing sin. When they said the words "we have strayed from thy ways like lost sheep, and there is no health in us; have mercy upon us, have mercy upon us, most merciful Father," he told me that he had a profound experience that he was in some mysterious sense "coming home." When he finally got back to his apartment, his wife asked, "Where have you been?" Once again he surprised himself by telling her, "I think I just became a Christian!" The next week the two of them attended the church, and not long after that they were baptized and publicly professed their faith in Christ.

In my experience, this kind of testimony to a divine power that seems to reach down and grab a person by surprise is not altogether a rare thing. And even when the encounter is not so dramatic, many of us have to admit that our coming to faith has a strong element of being drawn in against our own inclinations. So here, too, I find my Calvinism to fit the facts. To be sure, the teaching itself is based on the biblical texts about divine selectivity (for example, Acts 13:48—"and all who were appointed for eternal life believed") that we Calvinists insist on taking with utmost seriousness. But the teaching also conforms to the way things actually happen in the course of events.

Now, I understand how people can say that this pattern of God's selectivity does not seem fair. Why does he choose this person and not that one? Doesn't this make it all seem quite arbitrary? I understand this complaint, and I take it seriously. But frankly, it does not seem to be a complaint that is properly lodged against Calvinism in particular. It is better understood as a complaint about the facts of life. When a non-Calvinist Christian friend asks me how I can believe that God favors some people over others, it seems to me sufficient in many cases simply to point to the person's own life. Let's say that she was born in 1950 in Illinois, and that from her earliest days she was nurtured by the Christian community; they provided her with teachers and books and friends who encouraged her growth in the faith. In all of this, her life is much more privileged spiritually than, say, a person her own age who lives, say, in an isolated rural village in North Korea. And when my friend testifies to the grace of God in her life, she has no qualms about thanking the Lord for the special blessings that have been directed her way—blessings that are, in fact, missing in the life of her North Korean counterpart. Has Calvinism invented the notion of divine selectivity, or are we simply acknowledging something that seems to be really there in the way we experience our lives?

I don't mean to trivialize the concern. I worry much about the inequities in the human community—including the spiritual inequities. I hope my Calvinism does not stimulate a gloating attitude on my part. Later on I will elaborate on my concern about this temptation, a very real one for Calvinists in particular. The Lord may have chosen us, but certainly not with the intention of having us take glee in our chosen status. "Election" brings responsibility. But more on that further on.

THE *L:* A MISSION ACCOMPLISHED

In 1961 the Unitarians joined with the Universalists to form a new religious denomination called the Unitarian Universalist Association. Both groups had been around in America for quite a while—the Unitarians since 1825 and the Universalists since 1793—and each had developed its own unique theological perspective. When they got together, some clever commentator observed that the two different theologies formed an interesting new combination: the Universalists believed that God is too good to damn us and the Unitarians believed that we are too good to be damned.

I find nothing attractive in the Unitarian teaching as summarized in this piece of theological humor. But there is a certain logic to the Universalist part of the slogan. Indeed, some of the early Universalists made their case in self-consciously Calvinist terms. As one historian of the Universalist movement in America put it, the theology of the original Universalists "was, in essence, a radical form of Calvinism—one in which the concept of the elect was expanded to include all people."[15] These thinkers argued that, since we are all hopeless sinners, and since salvation can only come by grace alone, there is no reason to think that God will not save everyone in the end. After all, if we can't even believe in God apart from God's grace, why should God hold it against some people just because they don't believe in him?

These Universalists agreed with the traditional Calvinists that there is something wrong with believing that Christ died for all but that not all will be saved. The Calvinists, of course, had long countered that view with the insistence that, since not all are saved, Christ must not have died for all. The Universalists took it in a different direction. Since Christ *did* die for all human beings, they argued, this means that all human beings will be saved.

I think that, between the Calvinists and the Universalists, the Bible clearly supports Calvinism. But over against the other view—that

Christ died for all but that not all will be saved—we Calvinists do have to face up to some difficult biblical texts. When the biblical writers say on occasion that Christ died for "all," it really does look as though they mean that he died for *all*.

In the next chapter I'll spend a little time discussing some of the difficulties with the idea of limited atonement. For here I can just say that in the final analysis I stick with the **L** in TULIP. In all of these TULIP teachings it is important to keep a focus on the sovereignty of God. When Calvinists insist on the limited atonement idea, they mean to be pointing to the fact that a sovereign God could not have failed to accomplish what he set out to do in sending his only Son into the world. Jesus knew ahead of time whom he would save, and he set out to make their salvation a sure thing. There was no chance that he would die for people who would not accept his salvation. The success of the atonement—that those for whom Jesus died would arrive at their heavenly destination— was guaranteed from the outset. From the very beginning, he knew that his atoning work would be a mission accomplished.

THE *I:* A PURSUING GOD

There is no question in my mind that the TULIP doctrines all hang together. But they don't all "hang" in exactly the same way for me. Total depravity, for reasons I've already explained, is an *experienced* doctrine in my life. So is irresistible grace. Francis Thompson, the poet who wrote "The Hound of Heaven," was a Roman Catholic, but it does not surprise me that I have heard his lines most often quoted by Calvinists. He certainly captures my own experience when he describes his efforts to flee from the divine Pursuer:

> I fled Him, down the nights and down the days;
> I fled Him down the arches of the years;
> I fled Him down the labyrinthine ways
> Of my own mind; and in the mist of tears

I hid from Him, and under running laughter.
Up vistaed hopes I sped;
And shot, precipitated,
Adown titanic glooms of chasmèd fears,
From those strong Feet that followed, followed after.
But with unhurrying chase,
And unperturbèd pace,
Deliberate speed, majestic instancy . . .[16]

Again, that describes my own sense of how I have been saved. I feel "hounded" by God. The notion of a gracious pursuit I cannot resist, in spite of all of my efforts to do so, is more than a matter of doctrine for me. The doctrine arises out of my experience.

THE *P:* DIVINE FAITHFULNESS

I collect theological jokes, and one of my favorites was told to me many years ago by the historian Timothy Smith, a university professor who was also a Nazarene pastor. He advised me (with a twinkle in his eye) that I might want to use it to explain to people how we Calvinists believe that, since a person who is genuinely saved can never get un-saved, when a person looks as though they've fallen away from genuine salvation the likely explanation is that they were never really saved in the first place.

Here's the joke: Four theologians are standing alongside a train stopped between stations. They are looking at a dead body beside the tracks, arguing about what happened to the person. The Lutheran said he jumped from the train and was killed by the fall. The Catholic said he must have been pushed. The Methodist insisted he fell accidentally. But the Calvinist said that if he was really *off* the train, then he had never been *on* it in the first place!

I once knew a person I considered to be an exemplary Christian. I can still remember some important lessons he taught me about how to understand my relationship to God. But then some strange things happened in his personal life, and he cut himself off from both the church and his previous circle of Christian friends.

Did he lose his salvation? I don't know for sure. As a Calvinist who adheres to the *P* in TULIP, I only have two alternatives in explaining what happened. Either he had never been a person of faith, or he had a true faith that will someday surface again in his life. What I cannot say and still maintain my theological coherence is that he had true faith and then lost it completely.

Does it really matter how I explain the situation theologically? In one sense, no, it doesn't. I can pray for the person's salvation and leave it up to God to interpret my prayer—the Lord will know whether I'm asking for something brand-new or for a *re*-newal. Where the doctrine does matter is our own personal experience of a Love that will not let us go. The *P* is an important *spiritual* component of the Calvinist scheme. If you acknowledge your own total inability to save yourself and if you throw yourself on the mercy of a sovereign God, you need the *P* if you are to avoid the fears of divine arbitrariness.

The old Scottish preachers liked to tell a story about a woman who was known in her village for her abiding faith in Christ. She was now quite old and in poor health; it was clear she didn't have long to live. A young man regularly visited her, and as a spiritual seeker, he liked to quiz her about her Calvinist faith. One day he said to her, "Suppose after your long life of serving God and all of your praying and trusting—suppose that when you die, God sends you off to hell to suffer there forever."

"Don't you know your Bible better than that?" the woman replied. "If that were to happen, God would lose more than I would lose. I would lose my soul, which would indeed be terrible. But God would lose his *honor*. He has made precious promises to me. If he should fail to be faithful to his promises, his Word would be proven untrue. And the universe would end up in ruins!" The *P* in TULIP is not only about God's sovereignty; it is about his sovereign *faithfulness*.

During the 2000 United States presidential campaign, journalists had some fun at George W. Bush's expense over a silly little mistake he made on the campaign trail. Mr. Bush walked into a schoolroom where there was a large sign—meant to encourage the students in their studies—that read PERSEVERE. He misread it and launched into a discourse on how much he favored "preservation"—until one of his aides whispered in his ear, and Mr. Bush quickly changed the subject.

I have heard Calvinists propose substituting "preservation" for "perseverance" when explaining the *P* in TULIP. They find the "preservation of the saints" more God-honoring. I find their suggestion somewhat attractive. Once you get past the *T* in TULIP, the next three points feature God as agent: he elects, he provides the atonement, and he irresistibly draws us to himself. But suddenly at the end *we* seem to be the primary agent: *we* persevere in the Christian life.

Of course, there is a way of spelling it out so that the emphasis on human agency at the end actually provides a nice symmetry. TULIP begins with our total powerlessness, then it features three dimensions of God's activity on our behalf, and it ends with our being empowered—persevering—to live out our patterns of service. That's not a bad way of looking at the larger sequence of God's dealings with us!

Actually, though, I find both *P* words helpful in my spiritual life. We cannot persevere without God's preserving power. But his power is provided so that *we* do the persevering. Given all the complaints— not all of them completely off base—that Calvinism encourages a much too passive form of Christianity, it is helpful to hear a Calvinist call actively to persevere. But I do find it reassuring to know that the sovereign grace that saved me is also a preserving grace. The Lord is faithful.

chapter 4

A LOOK ON THE SHELF

I have a Mormon friend, a scholar, with whom I have some very interesting theological conversations. He doesn't fit my stereotype of what a Mormon should believe. He tells me, for example, that in recent years he has fallen in love with Paul's letter to the Romans. When I push him about what that love comes to, he says things that sound very good to me. At the heart of his relationship to God, he tells me, is his profound sense that he is a sinner who is saved by grace alone, with a salvation that is made possible only through the substitutionary atoning work of Jesus Christ at Calvary.

When he first said all of that to me, I asked him the obvious question: "But what about all those *other* things you believe as a Mormon— you know, that God started out as a finite human-like being, and that you are capable of being 'deified'?" He was quiet for a moment, and then he replied, "Well, I like to think of some of those uniquely Mormon beliefs as my shelf-doctrines. They are a part of my belief system, but they don't function in my life on a day-to-day basis. They certainly don't have the same role in my life as my deep sense that I am a sinner who is totally dependent on God's mercy. They are up there on my shelf, and when I have to, I take them down and use them. But for the most part they just sit there on the shelf."

His particular shelf-doctrines still worry me a lot—so we continue to have friendly arguments about them. But I do like his image.

Most of us who subscribe to a complex theological system have shelf-doctrines. I know I do. Indeed, at least one of the TULIP doctrines functions as a shelf-doctrine for me: the **L**. As I stated in the last chapter, I do believe it. It does seem to me to be a necessary element in the Calvinist system of thought, and if I have to defend it, I will. But I also find that I don't hold to it with the passion I have for the other Calvinist basics. It is there for me, but for the most part it just sits on my theological shelf. Since it has been one of the more troublesome Calvinist doctrines, though, I will take it off the shelf for a brief examination here.

A PARTICULAR REDEMPTION

Once, when I was a faculty member at Calvin College, I attended a conference where I struck up a conversation with a Baptist pastor. When he saw my institutional affiliation on my name tag, he said: "Oh, I'm a Calvinist too. Only four points, though!" I immediately guessed which one he was leaving out. He was a "TUIP" Calvinist.

The doctrine of the limited atonement has been the most debated of the TULIP teachings *within* the Calvinist camp, and there are more than a few Calvinists who, like the Baptist minister I just mentioned, simply reject it outright. There are understandable reasons why it has been so controversial. For one thing, although one can find some biblical support for it, it is not easy to square it with some of the language the Bible uses in describing the scope of Christ's atoning work. And how one comes down on the subject has important implications for the way in which one preaches the gospel to unbelievers.

The basic point of the doctrine of limited atonement is this: Since only some human beings are elected by God, the atoning work of Christ was accomplished to secure the redemption of those elect individuals. The Savior came to die for all those whom he intended to be saved; it is not the case that he died for all human beings.

Much of what makes this compelling for me is its relationship to the other Calvinist doctrines. In that sense, the doctrine of the limited atonement gains much of its force as a matter of logic. But there is also some strong biblical confirmation of the logic. At two places in Matthew's gospel, Jesus describes his mission in very focused terms: he will "give his life as a ransom for many" (Matthew 20:28), and his blood will be "poured out for many for the forgiveness of sins" (26:28)—a formulation echoed in Hebrews 9:28: "so Christ was sacrificed once to take away the sins of many people." And John's gospel seems to convey this teaching, as in: "All that the Father gives me will come to me, and whoever comes to me I will never drive away" (John 6:37). The same motif appears in Jesus' "high priestly" prayer in John 17, where he describes his almost-accomplished mission with reference to a specific subgroup of humankind: "Father, the time has come. Glorify your Son, that your Son may glorify you. For you granted him authority over all people that he might give eternal life to all those you have given him" (John 17:1–2). And he goes on to repeat the particularistic theme other times as well: "I have revealed you to those whom you gave me out of the world" (17:6); "I am not praying for the world, but for those you have given me, for they are yours" (17:9).

But then there are those passages that seem to be unqualified in their inclusiveness. When John the Baptist sees Jesus, he proclaims, "Look, the Lamb of God, who takes away the sin of the world!" (John 1:29). And, of course, there is the familiar message of John 3:16 and 17, that "God so loved the world that he gave his one and only Son" in order "to save the world through him." The writer to the Hebrews tells us that Jesus "suffered death, so that by the grace of God he might taste death for everyone" (Hebrews 2:9), and Paul writes that Christ's "one act of righteousness was justification that brings life for all men" (Romans 5:18).

THREE OPTIONS

Faced with these two apparently conflicting biblical formulations, we can do one of three things. One option is to take the inclusive wordings to be the more precise ones, and to interpret the particularistic in the light of the inclusive. That is the route followed by all non-Calvinists, as well as by the Calvinists of the "TUIP" variety. A second alternative is to take the particularistic texts to be the precise ones, and the inclusive ones to be looser formulations. Those who choose this option often argue, for example, that when biblical writers link Christ's atoning work to "all" or "everyone" or "the world," they do not mean to include each human individual; rather, they are indicating that the elect are drawn from many tribes and nations and classes of people.

There is a third option, and this is the one I take: I simply live with both sets of texts, refusing to resolve the tension between what looks like conflicting themes. This is not an altogether comfortable position for me. I would like to be much clearer on the subject, but I really do not know how to proceed further. I can honestly say I've made the effort. At the time I'm writing this, for example, I've just finished reading a lengthy book on the subject, *The Atonement Controversy in Welsh Theological Literature and Debate, 1707–1841,* by Owen Thomas. First published in 1874, it was recently translated from Welsh into English, and there is more than enough detail in these three-hundred-plus pages to satisfy anyone's curiosity about how Calvinists have argued among themselves about the limited atonement. Indeed, John Aaron, who did the important work of translating this volume, observes that Thomas was so thorough in his coverage of the debates that he included not only "practically everything of importance" but also, he adds in a candid parenthetical aside, "a good deal of the unimportant."[17]

Reading this account of these often acrimonious Calvinist debates was a good exercise for me. And I ended up pretty much where I started— albeit with much more information to reinforce my ambivalence. I found many examples of a Calvinism that was willing to live with the tensions on this subject. The author himself obviously favors this stance, since his account turns most positive when he is writing about times when most of the Calvinists could hold to "the specific appointing of Christ as Substitute for his people," while "with equal vigour they declared the infinite sufficiency of his sacrifice for all mankind in general and the sincere offer of the gospel for all to come to him for forgiveness and salvation."[18]

In highlighting the need to declare vigorously "the infinite sufficiency" of Christ's atoning work, Owen Thomas was pointing to a much-discussed topic in the intra-Calvinist debates. This emphasis was meant to counter the idea, put forth by some Calvinists, that Christ's sacrifice was a kind of quantitative transaction. The defenders of that approach spoke as though, as Andrew Fuller (who was critical of this viewpoint) characterized it, "the atonement of Christ were considered the literal payment of debt," so that "the measure of his sufferings were according to the number of those for whom he died, and to the degree of their guilt in such a manner as that if more had been saved, or if those who are saved had been more guilty, his sorrows would have been proportionately increased."[19] Fuller offered a more expansive portrayal, namely, that Christ's redemptive mission was carried out, "not on the principle of commercial, but of moral justice, or justice as it relates to *crime*." The "grand object" of Christ's atoning work, said Fuller, was "to express the divine displeasure against sin (Rom. 8:3) and so to render the exercise of mercy, in all the ways that sovereign wisdom should determine to apply it, consistent with righteousness (Rom. 3:25)." In this way, Christ's death was "in itself equal to the salvation of the whole world, were the whole world to embrace it." The atonement was not limited by "its insufficiency to save more than are saved, but in the sovereignty of its application."[20] In short, the death of Christ was sufficient to remove the penalty for sin *as such,* wherever and in whomever it resides. Having made full pardon possible through the work of the cross, it is God's own sovereign decision as to whom he will, according to his eternal counsel, extend that pardon.

A SPIRITUAL TONE AT STAKE

Well, what is the point of this kind of discussion? At the very least there is an important matter of emphasis—and of spiritual *tone*—at stake. Actually, it has always struck me that the **L** in TULIP contains the one odd adjective of the lot. The other four adjectives have a somewhat expansive feel to them: "total," "unconditional," "irresistible," "persevering." And then right in the middle the Calvinists plunk down the word "limited." Not that this disproves the doctrine—if the atonement is limited, so be it. But surely there is something wrong with giving the impression that the one important thing we want to emphasize about the atoning work of Jesus Christ is that it is "limited." This certainly does not capture my mood when I reflect on what Jesus accomplished in his atoning work. In my best moments I like to sing about the *magnitude* of the work of the cross in two senses. One is the magnitude of what it means to me personally. Here Charles Wesley puts it so well in a hymn he wrote:

> And can it be that I should gain an interest in the Savior's blood?
> Died he for me, who caused his pain,
> for me, who him to death pursued?
> Amazing love! how can it be
> that thou, my God, shouldst die for me?

The other is the expansive scope of what was accomplished for the larger creation, as expressed magnificently in Isaac Watts's carol:

> He comes to make his blessings flow
> far as the curse is found,
> far as the curse is found,
> far as, far as the curse is found.

Again, this is not to deny the doctrine of the limited atonement. I will still take it off the shelf on occasion and make use of it. But in doing so,

I will not try to force all of what I read in the Bible—or even all that I sing about—into a strict conformity with that teaching. I like the playfulness exhibited by one of the Welsh preachers who took part in a debate described by Owen Thomas. He urged his fellow Calvinist preachers to try to be a little more "careless" in interpreting the Bible. Not that he was recommending "the carelessness of levity," he quickly explained, "but rather the carelessness of faith." Many a Calvinist colleague, he observed, "will spend an hour's exegesis upon the word 'world'; it will almost take his breath away to utter 'all'; he will circumnavigate land and sea to avoid meeting 'everyone'." But the fact is, he went on, the Bible uses the words "all" and "world" in a fairly straightforward manner. "Trust more in the Bible, I implore you," he concluded.[21]

I try to live in the spirit of this trusting "carelessness of faith." Calvinism points me to the reality of a sovereign God whose ways are infinitely higher than our human minds can grasp. In the final analysis, in dealing with many of these mysterious things, all I can do is acknowledge God's sovereign purposes, while at the same time reminding myself that this God calls me to be obedient to those things that are clearly within my grasp to understand. Deuteronomy 29:29 is a much-quoted verse in the Calvinist tradition, and I quote it a lot to myself: "The secret things belong to the LORD our God, but the things revealed belong to us and to our children forever, that we may follow all the words of this law."

A "FREE OFFER"?

The **L** in TULIP has been the focus of another controversy, one closely related to the one we've just been discussing but with much more practical implications. This is the "free offer of the gospel" question. Can Calvinists consistently and with a good conscience say to any and all human beings that God wants them to repent and to accept Christ?

This question has been fiercely debated in just about every context where Calvinism has flourished. Indeed, it has probably stirred up more passions than any other theological topic within the Calvinist camp, with the anti-free-offer Calvinists accusing their counterparts of departing from the true faith, and their opponents depicting their critics as fanatical "hyper-Calvinists."

One of the more public outbreaks of this particular controversy occurred during Charles Spurgeon's ministry. Spurgeon was regularly attacked by his Calvinist critics, who condemned him for his "whoso-ever will may come" preaching.[22] Spurgeon was uncompromising in his response. He confessed that he did not know how the atonement could be limited to the elect and yet freely offered to all. But, he insisted, this he did know: that Christ does indeed freely offer salvation to all who will come to him. And he was convinced that this conviction was confirmed by the results of his preaching: "I know that the Lord has blessed my appeals to all sorts of sinners, and none shall stay me in giving free invitations as long as I find them in this Book."[23]

But the hyper-Calvinists with whom Spurgeon sparred would have nothing of that. Even though it might be literally correct from their point of view to make the offer conditionally to an unbeliever, as in, "*If you truly repent and ask for forgiveness in the name of Jesus, then* God will save you"—because, after all, from the Calvinist point of view the only ones who *will* truly repent are the ones who were predestined to eternal life—they nonetheless find such language dangerous. As one theologian of this persuasion put it, we must avoid any way of evangelizing that "leaves the impression, directly or by implication, that [God] is impotent to save unless the sinner first wills and gives his consent." You can do this, he says, "directly by the denial of predestination," or you can do it "indirectly, when preachers change the grace of God into an offer of God to all. . . . It is done in various forms and degrees. But all such preaching . . . finally leaves the impression that it is . . . all up to man, to the sinner, whether Jesus shall save him or not."[24]

I am not convinced. Here too I want to follow the Welsh preacher's advice to be a little "careless" in my reading of the Bible. When I come upon the apostle Paul writing to Timothy that God "desires everyone to be saved and to come to the knowledge of the truth" (1 Timothy 2:4 NRSV), it seems obvious to me at first glance that he really does mean *everyone*. But then I read some Calvinist theologians who want me to understand that "everyone" here refers to *every one of the elect*. I understand the theological impulses that push them to this interpretation, but I cannot buy their argument. I like the way Spurgeon put it: "I do not think I differ from any of my Hyper-Calvinistic brethren in what I do believe, but I differ from them in what they do not believe. I do not hold any less than they do, but I hold a little more, and, I think, a little more of the truth revealed in the Scriptures."[25]

My uncle Tunis Mouw had a wonderful career as a Baptist preacher who was passionate about evangelism. Soon after I became convinced of Calvinist theology, I told him about my newfound theological convictions, expecting him to argue with me a bit. But instead he told me he also was a convinced Calvinist. "But the way I see it," he said to me, "we have to paint above the door of salvation the words 'Whosoever will may come.' I hope, though, once a repentant sinner walks through that door, he will look up and see that the Lord has written on the other side, 'You have not chosen me, but I have chosen you.'"

This still strikes me as the right way for a Calvinist to view things.

TIME TO START SINGING

Having said that, I am at least capable of getting into a shelf-doctrine argument about the Timothy passage. But there is another scene in Scripture where, for me, argumentation is no longer appropriate. The event—Jesus' grieving over the city of Jerusalem—is recorded by both Matthew and Luke: "O Jerusalem, Jerusalem," Jesus cries out, "you who kill the prophets and stone those sent to you, how often I have longed to gather your children together, as a hen gathers her chicks under her wings, but you were not willing!" (Luke 13:34). Here God draws near as a sorrowful Savior to a rebel people. "I have longed to gather you," he calls out, "but you were not willing!"

This picture must somehow be incorporated into my understanding of God's sovereign dealings with humankind. I know of no appropriate response but the one Paul gives in Romans 11 as he comes to the end of his efforts to grasp God's ways with the Jewish people. Having struggled to make a coherent case, he seems suddenly unable to go any further. So he breaks forth with a hymn:

> Oh, the depth of the riches of the wisdom and knowledge of God!
> How unsearchable his judgments,
> and his paths beyond tracing out!
> "Who has known the mind of the Lord?
> Or who has been his counselor?"
> "Who has ever given to God,
> that God should repay him?"
> For from him and through him and to him are all things.
> To him be the glory forever! Amen.
>
> *Romans 11:33–36*

Sometimes it is important to know when the moment has arrived to stop thinking about the mysteries and simply to start singing.

chapter 5

NOT A STRANGER

I wish I could talk now with Lewis Smedes about the mysteries of God's purposes in the world. He and I often argued about God's sovereignty. The last argument we had on the subject was at one of our regular breakfast meetings just a month before he died. Now he has a whole new perspective on the issue.

DISCUSSIONS OVER BREAKFAST

Lew and I had known each other for over thirty years, and our friendship thrived on theological debate. He liked to get together for breakfast at a restaurant, and typically he would pose some theological problem he wanted to discuss. Our most sustained discussions kept coming down to questions about God's sovereignty. The arguments were always friendly ones—but they could get quite heated. Lew would often get irritated with me because he thought I was too quick to defend the Calvinist party line on the subject. And he knew that party line well. He had received his early seminary training in a setting where there was little tolerance for people who departed from traditional Dutch Calvinism. Later he had gone on to study with some of the best-known Reformed theologians in Europe.

I often wondered how much we really disagreed. Lew always came at the issue with a passionate commitment to real people. He would talk about attempting to comfort a couple who had lost a teenage son in a car accident. They had asked him why God would allow this kind of thing to happen, and he had responded by telling them that the death of their son was *not* the will of God. "I refuse to say that God ordains a tragedy like that, Richard," he would say to me in an anguished voice. "I'm not even going to say that God *permitted* it to happen. God *hates* it when people lose a son whom they dearly love!"

It was hard to argue with that. I would tell him how much I appreciated his pastoral approach in a situation of that sort. Like him, I would not simply tell the couple that God had his own mysterious reasons for allowing this to happen and that they ought to resign themselves to the will of their sovereign Lord. I too believe that God grieves with us when we experience our deepest losses.

But I still wanted to push Lew on what I saw as an important point of theology. "Let's agree that it's not a good pastoral strategy to rehearse the basic doctrines of Calvinism with people who are desperately grieving. But do we really want to tell them that God is *not* in control of the universe—that the Lord is completely *helpless* when it comes to traffic accidents?" My tone too would get quite passionate. "And what about a couple I know who had a very different way of dealing with their grief? They said that in their deep sorrow they knew their only comfort was to trust that the Lord had some purpose in allowing the accident. What are you going to tell them? That God is clueless on matters of this sort?"

"Not clueless," was Lew's reply. "And not helpless. He will not allow these things to defeat his ultimate purposes, which are *good* purposes. But that he *ordained* it, or even that he *permitted* it—no, this I cannot say."

"Well, I'm not always going to say it either," I would retort. "And I will often find it impossible even to think it. But neither can I bring myself to say the opposite—that things happen which are outside of God's control or contrary to his ultimate purposes."

And the argument would go on.

Lew Smedes wasn't just being cantankerous. He was getting at issues that should continue to bother every Calvinist. Now that he is gone, I have to find new ways to make sure I'm bothered by them.

Lew was raising from within a Calvinist perspective the questions that lead many other Christians to form a rather negative impression of Calvinism as such. They see this emphasis on God's sovereign control over all things as encouraging a passive, fatalistic spirit. If God's purposes are unfathomable, then shouldn't we just quietly accept whatever comes to pass? Why spend a lot of time trying to figure out the mysteries? And even worse, doesn't this theology come off as rather cruel in very real pastoral situations? Doesn't it have the effect of making people feel guilty about asking urgent questions that arise out of the deep places in their souls?

I am basically with Lew Smedes in viewing the practical issues, even though his way of formulating the theological answers about God's sovereignty made me nervous. I do think that it takes hard work to reconcile a belief in God's sovereign purposes with what actually happens in our lives. I have no use for a glib set of answers to deeply felt questions. Being a Calvinist should involve spiritual *struggle* as we do the best we can to come to terms with the fact that God's judgments are unsearchable.

The problem with the kind of argument Lew Smedes and I liked to have is that we often assume we have only two options. Either God ordains/permits everything that comes to pass, and we simply have to accept that fact, or there are some things that happen even though God does not want them to. There is at least one other option, and it is the one I want to argue for: God ordains/permits everything that comes to pass, but we *don't* simply have to accept that fact. We can complain to God rather vigorously about the things we have a hard time accepting.

"WHAT MORE CAN HE SAY?"

One of my college students came to me after class one day to talk about her religious struggles. It was a Monday morning, and she was still upset about some lines from a familiar hymn the congregation had sung at the end of the worship service she had attended the day before:

> How firm a foundation, ye saints of the Lord,
> Is laid for your faith in His excellent Word!
> What more can He say than to you He hath said,
> To you who for refuge to Jesus have fled?

"In the sermon the preacher had made it all sound so neat and tidy," the student reported. "And I was sitting there seething, because I had all these questions that weren't being answered. And then we sang that line—'What more can He say than to you He hath said?' I just felt like standing up and screaming, 'God could say a lot more! A *lot* more! I have too many questions, and I am not getting the answers!'"

I certainly did not have the answers to her questions. And I do like that hymn. But I did encourage her to keep asking the questions—and to keep asking them directly of God. Indeed, I told her, the Bible gives us permission to challenge the Almighty. The writers of the psalms regularly address difficult questions to the Lord.

The biblical psalms are an important part of my spiritual life. I read them—I pray them—regularly. I do so because they capture the full range of my spiritual moods. And I am convinced that a willingness to express these various moods is an important way of honoring a central Calvinist tenet: the sovereignty of God. More important, it is a way of honoring the biblical message.

One thing I like about the introduction of praise songs into worship in recent times is that this kind of music has brought back the singing of the psalms to the Christian community. Singing or chanting the biblical psalms has a long history in Christian worship, but the practice has been in decline in many parts of the church for a while. A good portion of the contemporary praise songs are, in fact, passages from the psalms set to music. And this is a good thing.

I worry about the fact, though, that typically only the "praise" psalms are being sung these days. We also need the psalms of lament, where the psalmists often complain about God, addressing God directly with their challenges. Here is an example:

> How long, O LORD? Will you forget me forever?
>   How long will you hide your face from me?
> How long must I wrestle with my thoughts
>   and every day have sorrow in my heart?
>   How long will my enemy triumph over me?
>
> *Psalm 13:1–2*

And here is one that contains more than a hint of irritation—even sarcasm:

> Awake, O Lord! Why do you sleep?
>   Rouse yourself! Do not reject us forever.
> Why do you hide your face
>   and forget our misery and oppression?
>
> *Psalm 44:23–24*

The writers of these psalms had a clear notion of God's sovereignty. They knew that God does not fall asleep. They knew that God is all-knowing and everywhere present. But horrible things were happening in the world, things that clearly violated God's revealed will for humankind. How could God stand by and do nothing? Why was God not acting to eliminate these evils? And so the psalmists challenged God: *Lord, if you are who you say you are, what is keeping you from acting on our behalf?*

The psalmists would agree with my college student friend. What more can God say to us about his purposes in the world? Well, frankly, a *lot* more!

LEARNING FROM THE RABBIS

I know this kind of talk will strike many Christians as lacking in proper spiritual humility. But I think their reaction points to a serious defect in much of recent Christian spirituality. This is why I often learn more from Jewish writers on a proper way of acknowledging God's sovereignty than I do from Christian thinkers. In some important ways, they are better Calvinists than many Calvinists I know!

I have been especially helped in this regard by David Wolpe's wonderful little book titled *The Healer of Shattered Hearts: A Jewish View of God,* where Rabbi Wolpe offers many intriguing insights about God's sovereignty from the rabbinic tradition. He points out, for example, that in Jewish thought the willingness to accuse God of various things—like sleeping on the job or being insensitive to human suffering—is actually an expression of a sense of profound *intimacy* between God and human beings.[26] He illustrates this with the example of Abraham's efforts to try to convince God to spare the city of Sodom from destruction. In this conversation—"surely the most presumptuous round of bargaining on record," Wolpe observes—Abraham even resorts to a bit of taunting: "Shall the Judge of all the earth not do justice?" he asks God (Genesis 18:25).[27]

This kind of "audacity still surprises a reader of the biblical story," says Wolpe. After all, if God is sovereign—if he really is "the Judge of all the earth"—then shouldn't Abraham submit unquestioningly to God's stated plan?

To put it this way, says Wolpe, is to miss a basic point about God's sovereignty: God is the Author of the standards he asks us to uphold. He is the One who tells *us* to be just and faithful and merciful:

> To assume that we may not question God is to assume that we have no real handle on what is good. Since all of religion presupposes that we have some knowledge of the good, we have the right to hold the Author of ethical norms to the same norms

Himself. God cannot escape His own pronouncements. He is Judge of all the earth. He must do justice.[28]

Many of the traditional rabbis took this business of questioning God pretty far. Here is a fascinating example offered by Wolpe. A much-revered rabbi once stood before the ark of the covenant, getting ready for the opening service of *Yom Kippur,* the Day of Atonement. The opening prayer had to begin exactly at sunset, and the rabbi waited silently for the right moment. He seemed to be deep in thought, and the people gathered for worship started to worry that he might not begin on time. But then he spoke:

> "Dear God," he said, "we come before You this year, as we do every year, to ask Your forgiveness. But in this past year, I have caused no death. I have brought no plagues upon the world, no earthquakes, no floods. I have made no women widows, no children orphans. God, You have done these things, not me! Perhaps You should be asking forgiveness from me."
>
> The great Rabbi paused, and continued in a softer voice, "But, since You are God, and I am only Levi Yitzhak, *Yisgadal v'yiskadah sh'mei rabah* [Magnificent and sanctified is Thy Name]," and he began the service.[29]

Again, this may strike many Christians as pushing things a bit too far with God. But it is important to discern the spiritual impulses at work here. The line between blasphemy and issuing challenges to God out of deeply pious motives may be a thin one. But the rabbi has not crossed it here. He is not mocking God in an irreverent manner. Like Abraham, he is taking seriously what God has actually revealed about his own divine nature. God has told us that he is supremely faithful and merciful. He has announced to us that he is a God of justice who requires his people to do justice and to love mercy. When, out of genuine anguish of soul, we ask the Lord how his actions—or the seeming lack of action on his part—are to be reconciled with his own publicly proclaimed attributes, we are addressing him as his intimate ones, people who want desperately to love him and to understand his will for our lives.

We do not dishonor God if we struggle honestly with questions about how we are to best understand his self-revelation. It is not insulting to him if we sincerely express our puzzlement and frustrations in his presence. But because we also know that he is sovereign—and that he does not have to justify his ways to us—we must eventually get around to the praise songs.

SEEING THE FACE IN TRAGEDY

I read a story in a book by a Dutch theologian who had served awhile as a pastor in a small rural village in the Netherlands. During his pastorate a terrible tragedy struck—one that deeply affected the lives of several families in his Calvinist congregation. He met with a group of them and attempted to bring comfort. But in the course of doing so he also expressed his own inability to explain the sort of tragedy they had experienced. One of the church members interrupted him with this comment: "Minister, no stranger did that to us."

The theologian who told this story was using it to illustrate what it means to have an abiding faith in God. The "face" they were seeing in this tragedy, he said, was "not the real face; behind it [was] hidden the friendly face of God."[30] These villagers were obviously deeply distressed at the tragedy that had occurred. They knew what their pastor was getting at in expressing his own puzzlement. They too were wondering how the Lord could allow this kind of thing to happen to them. But they wanted to be clear about the basics. It was no stranger who had done this to them. It was the God whom they worshiped and trusted. Their faith in a loving God was being tested, but it was not being undermined. They would have understood the point that Rabbi Wolpe makes just after telling the story about the rabbi who accused

God on the Day of Atonement and then went on to offer his prayerful praise to the Lord:

> That [continuing to pray] is the final answer. There is no escaping the pain of suffering and the tormenting questions of God's silence. In the end, however, the Jewish position has always been to understand that, however close, there is a gap between human beings and God, and we cannot finally understand His intentions or design.
>
> Therefore we continue to pray.[31]

GOD AS BULLY?

To be sure, Christians *do* want to say something more. We do not end up at exactly the same place as our Jewish friends.

When I was a graduate student in philosophy, I had a professor who was virulently anti-Christian. Of course, most of my professors were non-Christians, but this one was aggressively *anti*-Christian. While he had long ago abandoned the faith of his childhood, he was not content to ignore religious questions, or to discuss them calmly. He saw it as his mission to try to convince his students of the evils of the biblical perspective.

He loved to talk about the book of Job, and he was eloquent in his unique retelling of the story. He would follow the traditional narrative for the most part, but when he got near the end, he introduced his own spin. Job, he said, asked God why he had allowed Job and his family to experience such profound suffering. Instead of giving him a reasonable answer, my professor said, God just starts to boast about his power. The professor made much of God's speech in chapters 40 and 41, where the Lord points out that he created the mighty creatures of the earth. The behemoth is so strong that no human being can tame it; only "his Maker can approach him with his sword" (Job 40:19). And the leviathan of the deep: "Can you make a pet of him like a bird or put him on a leash for your girls?" the Lord asks Job rhetorically (41:5). But he, the mighty God, can tame this awesome beast, even though "nothing on earth is his equal—a creature without fear" (41:33).

Here is what the Lord is doing, my professor insisted. He is putting on a show of power. He is a Big Bully, pounding his chest. Job has presented him with a reasonable request, and all God can say in response is, "I'm bigger than you are! Can you do *this?* Can you? And can you do *this?*"

Then my professor got to his punch lines. In the end, Job heaves a big sigh and says, "Okay, you win. You *are* bigger than I am. I give up!" And then the Devil catches Job's eye and winks at him. And Job winks back. They both know the answer now: Humor the Big Bully.

UNDERSTANDING THE DIVINE SILENCE

Now, depicting God as a Big Bully *is* blasphemy. But in a perverse way it does point to something important in the Job story. God really does not answer Job. He really does point to his own power rather than directly responding to Job's questions. And in a profound sense, that is the best God can offer in the Old Testament context.

The situation changes, however, in the New Testament. To be sure, when we read the gospel account we are no further along in actually getting answers to the sorts of questions raised by the story of Job. But God does respond in a way that goes far beyond anything Job could comprehend. God sends his only begotten Son into the world. Jesus enters into our condition. He is tempted in the ways we are tempted. He suffers in the ways we suffer. And because of his earthly ministry, we have a Savior who can "sympathize with our weaknesses" and who "has been tempted in every way, just as we are—yet was without sin" (Hebrews 4:15).

Jesus went to Calvary and suffered a horrible death on our behalf, bearing our sins in his own body. And when he cried out on the cross, "My God, my God, why have you forsaken me?" there was no answer. The Father was silent.

The silence of heaven at Calvary was not, however, the silence of indifference. Jesus was not abandoned by a Bully God who did not care about what was happening on the cross. The silence of heaven was of a very different sort.

C. S. Lewis made the right distinction in discussing his own despair when his wife died of cancer. He filled several notebooks with questions and complaints addressed to God. He struggled with the fact of divine sovereignty and human suffering in a very focused manner. Finally, though, he comes to a resolution of sorts:

> When I lay these questions before God I get no answer. But a rather special sort of "No answer." It is not the locked door. It is more like a silent, certainly not uncompassionate, gaze. As though He shook His head not in refusal but waiving the question. Like, "Peace, child; you don't understand."[32]

What Lewis says here can also help us grasp something about the silence of God the Father at Calvary. If we take the mission of the suffering Savior seriously, we have the answer to my philosophy professor. Yes, God does not answer Job. Nor does he always answer our own cries of anguish. In the Old Testament, the only thing God could do, in lieu of answering the questions, was to point to his own sovereign power. But in the redemptive mission of Christ, God takes an important further step. He demonstrates his compassion to us. He tells us, in so many words, that whatever else we might wonder about his purposes, we have no good reason to think that he is the Big Bully. Because he finally came down himself and suffered with us, for us. And here he does really ask us, "Can you do *this*? Can you?" And in this case the "this" is his going to the cross, experiencing in his own person the cursedness of our sin and our suffering.

Jerry Sittser, religion professor at Whitworth College, puts it much better than I can. Jerry and three of his children survived a horrible accident in which Jerry lost his mother, his wife, and a young daughter. His book about how he wrestled for a long time—spiritually and theologi-cally—with this loss is the most profound book on grieving I have ever read. Jerry is a Calvinist, and before the accident he had been firmly con-vinced of God's sovereignty. After the accident, though, the sovereign God seemed very distant:

> My loss made God seem terrifying and inscrutable. For a long time I saw his sovereignty as a towering cliff in winter—icy, cold, and windswept. . . . It loomed over me, completely obliv-ious to my presence and pain. . . . I yelled at God to acknowl-edge my suffering and to take responsibility for it, but all I heard was the lonely echo of my own voice.[33]

When he finally made his peace with God's sovereignty, it was by dis-covering new meaning in the sufferings of Jesus:

> The Incarnation means that God cares so much that he chose to become human and suffer loss, though he never had to. I have grieved long and hard and intensely. But I have found comfort in knowing that the sovereign God, who is in control of everything, is the same God who has experienced the pain I live with every day. No matter how deep the pit into which I descend, I keep finding God there.[34]

"DOING SOMETHING"

I admire these people—the rabbi who talked about the need to forgive God, C. S. Lewis, Jerry Sittser—who struggle with their belief in God's sovereignty. Their way strikes me as more biblically faithful than the posture of passive fatalism. Their way seems to me to be essential to a healthy Calvinism.

Once when there was a specific racial crisis going on in the city where I lived, a group of us—Christians from a variety of denominations—got together to talk about how we might respond as believers who were committed to interracial healing. Someone suggested that we hold an interdenominational prayer service, and several of us thought it was an excellent idea. One young activist, though, dissented. "I don't want to just pray," he said in an anguished voice, "I want us to *do* something!"

I agreed that we should not "just pray." There were other actions we also needed to take. But I disagreed with his theological assumptions about prayer. Prayer *is* doing something. It is petitioning the Ruler of the universe. It is making our case in the Final Court of Appeals.

When Abraham argued with God, he was *doing* something. So were the psalmists when they lamented the injustice and oppression they saw all around them.

Prayers of petition and complaint are an important part of my Calvinist spirituality. I get in moods of despair when I wonder what in the world the Judge of all the earth could have in mind when he allows the things he seems to tolerate. In those situations, I feel I have no other choice but to *do something.* I argue with God. I pray those psalms that allow me to bring my complaints before the throne of the Almighty. I seldom get answers when I do all this. But I do sense the need to express my concerns and make my case.

But there's another thing I've also learned to do. I look at the cross. I see Jesus suffering. I hear his own despair. I hear again the Son of God use a psalm of anguished lament—"My God, my God, why have you forsaken me?"—as he cries out in utter abandonment and desolation (Matthew 27:46). And when I remind myself of what happened at Calvary, I know in the deep places that God's "no answer" is not a shutting of the door but a compassionate, sorrowful gaze. Then, after a while— sometimes it takes quite a while—I can sing praise songs again.

WHAT DOES GOD KNOW ABOUT LOSS?

I read a story recently about a tragedy that occurred at a British sports event where a large number of people, most of them young men, were trampled to death. An official was meeting with anxious parents who had gathered to hear the names of those who had been killed. When he finished reading the list, he assured the parents that he personally, as a Christian, would be praying that God would bring them comfort. Out of the group came the anguished cry of a grieving father: "What does God know about losing a son?"

When I read that story, I thought about the time Lew Smedes told a grieving couple that God was grieving with them over the loss of their only son. And I thought about a striking phrase Jerry Sittser used to describe the God who sent his own Son to the cross. That God, Sittser said, is "a suffering Sovereign."[35]

Those Dutch villagers had it right. It may be impossible to understand God's purposes at many points in our lives. But it is no stranger we are dealing with.

chapter 6

AFTER THE ELECTION

The TULIP doctrines focus primarily on the salvation of individuals. And, as I have been arguing thus far, that focus, along with a spirituality of acknowledging God's control over all things, is what "mere" Calvinism basically is all about. When I first got excited about being a Calvinist, these are the things that grabbed me.

As I moved along in my journey though, I was confronted with new questions and challenges. As I have already testified, I eventually found the resources for dealing with these issues in the Calvinism I had already embraced. Building on the "mere," I discovered the "more" of Calvinist life and thought.

CALVINIST ACTIVISM IN WASHINGTON

In the fall of 1969 I participated in a "March on Washington" to protest the Vietnam War. Technically, I went as a journalist; my expenses were paid by a magazine that had asked me to write a report on the antiwar movement from the perspective of evangelical Christianity. But, truth be told, I was not there as an "objective" reporter. I joined into the activities as someone who was deeply disturbed about my country's involvement in what I believed was an unjust war.

Thousands of people marched, and they represented a wide variety of ideologies. At one point a group of radicals hoisted a Vietcong flag, and many of us booed. Some people were carrying American flags to signal the fact that they were protesting as people who loved their country. At various points along the line of march, I detected what was for me an unfamiliar smell—and then I overheard someone remark that she was "getting nauseated from all the marijuana smoke!" I saw a smattering of clerical collars, and even several nuns wearing the traditional habit.

In the midst of all this, while turning a corner I spied a small sign being carried by someone a half block ahead of me in the parade. It said, in dark-crayoned letters, "A Calvinist for Peace." I found a sidewalk where I could run ahead, and I greeted the sign-carrier. He was a lone student from Westminster Theological Seminary in Philadelphia. "I'm against the war," he told me, "but I wanted to witness to a very different understanding of peace than the views of the other marchers."

At that time in my life I hadn't yet thought at great length about what a distinctively Calvinist social activism might look like. I did know that the connection was worth exploring. I was aware, for example, that John Calvin believed that the gospel had clear social and political implications. And I had been discovering that many other Calvinists in the past had worked at formulating a vision for an active witness to the power of the gospel for all of life, including the more corporate dimensions of human interaction. But the very fact that I was taken aback by seeing a sign at an antiwar march proclaiming "A Calvinist for Peace" told me that I had some work to do in order to get clearer in my own mind about the connections between the basic TULIP perspective and a Calvinist understanding of how we are to serve the Lord as his active disciples in the world.

ELECTED *TO* SOMETHING

Here is a good place to start. Suppose a person is elected to be president of the United States and then spends the first year of his presidency talking a lot about the fact that he has been elected. In his talks to the nation, he tells us how thrilled he is that he—of all the people who might have been chosen for the job—was elected to the office of president. He commissions studies to find out exactly how he got elected. He regularly thanks those citizens who cast their votes for him. He also talks much about his predecessors—people before him who had been elected to the presidency—and tells us how privileged he considers himself to be counted in the company of such a distinguished group of elected officials.

Surely there would come a point where we would all urge him to think about an important question he seems to be ignoring: What were you elected *for*? What did we elect you to *do*?

I'm sure the parallel to Calvinism is obvious. It is not enough to *be* elected, and to rejoice in that fact. Divine election is *to* something. We are chosen by God to serve in an "office."

This is where we need to go a step beyond the TULIP doctrines. Those teachings focus on an important question: *How do fallen, hopelessly depraved human creatures get right with God?* And the shorthand answer is: *By sovereign grace.* But there is an important next question: *And what happens after we are made right with God?* And here too the answer centers on the notion of divine sovereignty: *God elects us to participate in a covenant community that shows forth his sovereign rule over all areas of life.*

PEOPLEHOOD AND GRITS

I once heard a Catholic priest, a native of New Jersey, give a homily in which he told about visiting the southern part of the United States for the first time. At the hotel restaurant on his first morning, he studied the breakfast menu. Several combination meals featured grits, so when the waitress came for his order, he asked her, "Miss, what is a grit?" She replied, "Honey, they don't come by *themselves!*"

The priest used this story to emphasize the importance of the body of Christ. Christians don't come by themselves, he said. Like grits, "Christian" is a plural thing. To follow Jesus is to be part of a community.

This is good theology for all of us. What the apostle Peter said to the members of the early church is also meant for us: we are "a chosen people, a royal priesthood, a holy nation. . . . Once [we] were not a people, but now [we] are the people of God" (1 Peter 2:9–10).

This peoplehood theme has typically been emphasized by Calvinists. Many in the Calvinist tradition have been particularly fond of the term "covenant community." This is especially true of folks in the Reformed and Presbyterian churches, where traditionally the TULIP doctrines have been seen as intimately linked to what is referred to as "covenant theology," to the insistence that God calls believers and their children into a special covenantal partnership. For the Reformed and Presbyterian types, this has been the basis of arguing in favor of infant baptism. But even many Baptist Calvinists—Spurgeon chief among them—have made the idea of a covenant community central to their preaching.

One benefit of this covenant theology often missed by critics of Calvinism is the way the idea of a covenantal relationship with God has often served to "soften" the idea of predestination. There is no denying that a belief that we are predestined to eternal life can lead to a deterministic, even fatalistic, understanding of the Christian life. If it is God who does the choosing, then we may be tempted to think that our own choosing, our own responding to God, is a charade. It is all preprogrammed.

But Calvinist theologians go out of their way to deny this implication. The problem, though, is that the denials, as theological statements, can seem abstract and formulaic. People can be told that their choices do matter, but when they also hear a lot about predestination, this message may not sink in very deep. When the idea of covenant is emphasized, however, the relationship between God and redeemed human beings takes on a different feel. Covenants are made between *partners*. In this case the partners are by no stretch of the imagination equal—but the partnership is a real one. There is a *transaction* between us and God. We agree to the conditions of the partnership, and God agrees to keep certain promises he makes to us. The covenant partnership is one of *fellowship*. It is characterized by *intimacy*.

All these things have in fact been emphasized by Calvinists. Because of this idea of covenant, then, what might otherwise strike us as a theology that treats us as preprogrammed robots actually comes across as a much "softer" and "warmer" understanding of the relationship between God and his people.

But I especially like the way the peoplehood theme also tells us that the mission to which God calls us is much larger than any of us can accomplish on our own. The God who elects us calls us to do his will, to follow a way of life set forth in the covenant requirements he provides for his people. I once heard an evangelical preacher say that, while the Old Testament emphasized a faith that was corporate and "this-worldly," the New Testament shifts to a way of life that is primarily individual and "heavenly minded." It is precisely this kind of dichotomy that is opposed by covenant theology. God did not shift his basic interests from the Old to the New Testaments. God chose ancient Israel to be a model to the rest of the human race as to what it means for a people to live in the world in obedience to the God who saved them. And that same plan extends to the New Testament church.

God does save us as individuals. But this does not mean that he wants us to live out our lives in isolation from a corporate involvement. We need to find our individual callings in the context of the larger calling of the Christian community to which we belong. So in order to be clear about what God wants each of us to do as individuals, we must also be sure to be clear about the larger mission of the *covenant people* of God, sustained by his sovereign grace.

BECOMING AGENTS

A historian of Scottish Presbyterianism writes about two stages in early Calvinist thought in Scotland. The first stage was characterized, he says, by the proclamation "None but Christ *saves*"—this was the way these Calvinists expressed their disagreement with what they saw as a "works righteousness" in the Roman Catholicism of their day. In the second stage, the theme was "None but Christ *reigns*." Here they began to work out the implications of their Calvinism for how they were to live their lives in obedience to the authority of their sovereign Lord.[36]

This is exactly the progression I am laying out here. The TULIP doctrines tell that we are saved by sovereign grace alone. But when we ask what we're saved *for,* we hear God's call to witness—by a covenant community—to his sovereign reign over all things. Having been *acted upon* by that sovereignty, we become *agents* of God's sovereign rule.

I spend quite a bit of my time in conversations with non-evangelicals—theologians, journalists, social commentators—talking about issues of society and culture. I find that such people often refer to "theocracy" in a disdainful tone of voice. They think of many conservative Christians—especially the folks they identify with the "Religious Right"—as "theocrats," and they make it clear that they seriously dislike that way of viewing things. I often agree, at least in part, with their criticisms on the level of attitude and behavior. Many evangelicals have a difficult time adjusting to a highly pluralistic culture, and we often come across as trying to impose our standards—which for us are explicitly connected to biblical revelation—on folks who do not share our worldview.

But I do bristle when theocracy *as such* gets a bad press. I am a theocrat. Theocracy means "the rule of God." I do believe that God rules over all things. "The earth is the LORD's, and everything in it, the world, and all who live in it" (Psalm 24:1). Everyone who believes in the God who actively reigns over his whole creation is a theocrat.

I hasten to add that this does not mean I want to impose "Christian culture" on everyone. God desires that people freely acknowledge his rule and that they freely offer their lives of obedience to him. Nothing is gained when we impose specifically Christian standards on people who do not acknowledge God as the ruler over all things. The Mennonites have a nice phrase. They say we are presently living "in the time of God's patience." That's right. Someday every knee will bow and every tongue will confess that Jesus is Lord. Unbelievers will be forced to acknowledge where the true authority resided all along. But that day—the Day of Judgment—has not yet come. So we are in a time of waiting, of longing for the day when the rule of God will be made obvious to all creatures. The Christian community is called here and now by God to be a witness to the larger world of what it is like to live our lives in open acknowledgment of God's sovereign rule over all things.

MY SPIRITUAL JOURNEY

When I was growing up in the evangelical world we regularly had "testimony meetings." We sometimes referred to these times of sharing the stories of our faith pilgrimages as "popcorn testimony" times. The leader would call on folks to stand up and talk about their relationship to Christ, and things would begin rather slowly. But after two or three people started it up, soon people would be popping up (the popcorn image) all over the congregation to give their testimonies.

A testimony is necessarily a shorthand version of one's pilgrimage. And in that sense it is very compact—we typically create a story line for our lives that is oversimplified. But still, it is helpful to organize our thoughts about how God has dealt with us thus far. Given all the emphasis in theology these days on the importance of "narrative," I'm surprised that the "testimony meeting" seems to have gone out of fashion.

Anyway, I have a testimony about my spiritual journey. I have gone through three stages in my understanding of who Jesus is. To begin with, from my earliest days I have thought of Jesus as my *Savior*. What the apostle Paul wrote to Timothy applies to me as well: "from infancy you have known the holy Scriptures, which are able to make you wise for salvation through faith in Christ Jesus" (2 Timothy 3:15). When I was a high school student, I walked down the aisle at the 1957 Billy Graham Crusade in New York City to bear witness to my faith in the only One who could save me. But that was a public affirmation of something I had known all along: that the most important thing any human being can experience is the loving embrace of the heaven-sent Savior.

During my college years I discovered a second dimension of the person of Jesus: his *lordship*. This recognition applied primarily to my growing interest in intellectual matters. I came to see that he is Lord of our minds. I'll never forget a chapel talk at the Christian college I attended, given by a visiting speaker, Frank Gaebelein, who was the headmaster of Stony Brook School, a prestigious Christian prep school.

His talk was titled "The Christian's Intellectual Life," and I still remember some of his remarks—although I don't need to rely on memory alone, since his talk was later published in a book of his essays. In contrast to the outlook of secular types, said Gaebelein, Christians must insist that "our intellectual life is infused with faith." But it does not mean that Christian intellectual activity is an easy thing. We must pay a price if we are to use our minds to glorify God. "And the price will not come down. It is nothing less than the discipline of self-restraint and plain hard work."[37]

Until that time I had pretty much seen academic work as a chore I had to complete in order to get a job someday. But now I began to think about the ways in which thinking—and the hard work of studying difficult subjects—could be done to glorify God and honor the Lord Jesus. Paul's mandate, in 2 Corinthians 10:5, that "we take captive every thought to make it obedient to Christ" came to take on special meaning for me, which it still does today.

Of course, Christ's lordship goes far beyond the contents of our minds. Everything we do—our daily occupations and preoccupations—belongs to him. What Frank Gaebelein said about our intellectual pursuits can be extended more broadly. All of our lives—work, play, love, friendship, finances—will be "infused with faith" if we truly acknowledge him as our Lord.

The third stage was a recognition of the *kingship* of Jesus Christ. This happened during my graduate school days, when I was drawn into a social activism but felt ill prepared by my evangelical upbringing to deal with this in Christian terms. The big issues of the day were racial justice and the war in Vietnam, and I struggled with what it means to be a Christian when dealing with such things. What if you are convinced—as I was—that some of our societal practices and laws at the time were unjust? What if you worry that your nation has made a mistake in getting into a specific war?

As I searched for answers, I wandered for a while theologically, briefly flirting with both liberal Protestantism's social gospel teachings and Roman Catholic social thought. I quickly discovered, however, that neither of those perspectives could satisfy me, either in my soul or my intellect.

Finally I discovered a form of Calvinism that struck me as a powerful way of dealing with the issues. It helped me see that when the Bible talks about the "kingdom" of God, it is not merely speaking poetically. Jesus is a real King who has real authority. And there are times when his authority conflicts with the values of the societies in which we live and the governments that exercise authority over us. When this happens, we must be loyal to the only Ruler who truly matters in the final analysis. The kind of Calvinism I discovered not only helped me to understand the kingship of Jesus; it also tied that kingship nicely with his roles as my Savior and my Lord.

HE CARES ABOUT THE STUFF OF OUR DAILY PURSUITS

Once when I spoke at a retreat for Christian university students, I was met at the airport by a student whose assignment was to drive me to the retreat site. As he drove he told me how eager he was to attend this event. "I've been doing nothing for several months but study, study, study!" he told me. "I've been so wrapped up with the books I haven't had any time for the things of the Lord."

I knew what he meant, and I was able to offer him my sympathy. The life of the scholar—student or teacher—can be very demanding. The academic calendar is crowded with deadlines; as soon as one three-hour exam is over, you have to start worrying about the twenty-page paper due in two weeks. I love the academic life; I cannot imagine doing anything that would be more rewarding. But I also know it is a severe taskmaster. At times "study, study, study" can be more than a human being can handle.

But for all of my sympathy, I still worry when I hear someone like my student driver draw a stark contrast between academic pursuits and "the things of the Lord." I can put my objection quite bluntly: The things that occupy us in an academic setting are *themselves* "the things of the Lord." If I could rewrite his complaint for him in proper theological terms, I would put it this way: "I've been so wrapped up with the books I haven't had any time for some of the *other* things of the Lord."

And it isn't just the academic life. God cares deeply about all the "stuff" of our daily pursuits: the things we deal with in our workplaces, in our friendships and family relationships, in our leisure-time activities. This is what the psalmist is proclaiming when he writes that "the earth is the LORD's, and everything in it" (Psalm 24:1).

That's the kind of thing I have learned to appreciate in acknowledging that Jesus Christ is not only my personal Savior but the Lord over all my thoughts and the Ruler over all spheres of life. My main teacher here has been one of the great Dutch leaders of the nineteenth century. His brand of Calvinism helped me put a number of key pieces in place in my understanding of what it means to honor the full authority of Jesus Christ.

I can't go any further in talking about a full-orbed Calvinism without being explicit about some of the lessons I've learned from my teacher from the Netherlands.

chapter 7

EVERY SQUARE INCH

I am a "Kuyperian" Calvinist. That means I owe much—especially about the broader implications of Calvinism—to Abraham Kuyper, who was born in the Netherlands in 1837 and died in 1920.

Kuyper had an amazingly productive life. He founded two newspapers and wrote regularly for them throughout his career. He served for a while as a pastor. He established a major political party, which he led for many years in the Dutch parliament, and even served a term around the turn of the century as prime minister of the Netherlands. He founded the Free University of Amsterdam, where he often taught theology. He led a number of congregations out of the historic Dutch Reformed church, forming a new denomination, the second largest in the Netherlands.

Kuyper published many books and essays dealing with a wide variety of topics in theology and social thought. In 1898 he visited the United States, delivering the famous Stone Lectures at Princeton Theological Seminary. These lectures are still in print, and they provide an excellent overview of his thinking.[38] He continues to have an important influence today, especially among evangelical scholars.[39]

CONNECTING WITH "THE LITTLE PEOPLE"

Abraham Kuyper always made a point of staying connected to those he referred to as "the little people," the ordinary Christians who were not well educated but who had a deep commitment to Christ's kingdom. Even though he greatly valued scholarship, he wanted to promote a kind of Calvinism that would inspire people in all walks of life to glorify God in every area of service.

His love of the common folks went deep, and it flowed from gratitude for the ways in which very ordinary Christians had taught him some important spiritual lessons. Kuyper had studied for the ministry at the University of Leiden, where the prestigious faculty was steeped in the liberal theology that was trendy among Christian intellectuals at the time. Kuyper bought into this liberalism, and when he began his ministry, he had no appreciation for Calvinist orthodoxy.

In his first pastorate, however, he encountered some church members who exhibited a vibrant evangelical faith grounded in the TULIP doctrines. One of them was Pietje (pronounced "Peet-ya") Baltus, a young woman, the daughter of a miller. Pietje's warm Calvinist faith was nurtured by her involvement in a "house church" type of fellowship, and she boycotted Kuyper's worship services because of the content of his preaching. When Kuyper went to visit her, she refused to shake his hand—which was an unmistakable signal to Kuyper that she rejected his pastoral authority.

In that culture the Dutch Reformed minister was an important figure, deserving of great respect, so Kuyper had every reason to be offended by her gesture. But, much to his own surprise, he wasn't. Instead, he felt a genuine curiosity about the convictions that motivated her. He asked her questions and continued to meet with Pietje and her friends—all of them uneducated peasant folk—listening carefully to their testimonies. Here is how he put it later in his life:

> I did not set myself against them, and I still thank my God that I made the choice I did. Their unwavering persistence has been a blessing for my heart, the rise of the morning star in my life. In their simple language, they brought me to that absolute conviction in which alone my soul can find rest—the adoration

and exaltation of a God who works all things, both to do and to will, according to his good pleasure.[40]

This experience led Kuyper to an evangelical faith, which in turn generated a passionate commitment to traditional Calvinist theology. But he ever thereafter also placed a strong emphasis on the need for a very personal relationship with God. Indeed, one of his favorite Bible verses was Psalm 73:28: "But as for me, it is good to be near God. I have made the Sovereign LORD my refuge; I will tell of all your deeds." He even took the phrase "near unto God" as the title for the book containing many of biblical meditations he wrote throughout his busy public career.[41] In these meditations, Kuyper constantly emphasized the need for the individual believer to turn away from the demands of the active life and retreat into that very private sacred space where the soul is alone with its Maker.

BEFORE THE FACE OF GOD IN THE DOG-EAT-DOG WORLD

Abraham Kuyper made much of the fact that we are also in God's presence in our *public* lives. One of his favorite Latin phrases was *coram deo*—which means "facing God," or "being before the face of God." In every area of our lives, Kuyper proclaimed, we live *coram deo*. In addition to his celebration of the intensely private experience of a Savior's love, he also placed a strong emphasis on the supreme rule of Jesus Christ over all spheres of creaturely life. Kuyper's followers are fond of quoting the manifesto he issued at Free University's inaugural convocation: "There is not a square inch in the whole domain of our human existence over which Christ, who is sovereign over *all,* does not cry: 'Mine!'"[42]

The practical meaning of the *coram deo* emphasis was brought home to me nicely once by a friend of mine, an insurance agent, who saw Kuyper as one of the key influences on his understanding of his Christian calling. He appeared on a local TV program where several businesspeople talked about how their Christian convictions influenced their daily work. One of them told how he had arranged with his secretary to keep one noon hour a week free of any appointments. "During that one hour," he said, "I like to get out of the dog-eat-dog world of business and shut my office door, taking out my Bible to spend some time alone with my Lord." My friend was the next to speak. "I do that kind of thing too," he reported, "but I also think a lot about how I am with my Lord *in* the dog-eat-dog world of business!" He went on to tell about a young married couple who came to his office recently to work on their insurance needs. "They will be dealing with some of the most important issues in their lives," my friend said. "What it means to be secure. What their priorities will be as they plan the future of the family they wanted to have. I had a real sense that my Lord was looking over my shoulder as I wrote a policy for them!" *Coram deo.* Kuyper would have been pleased.

WORLDVIEW AND TRANSFORMATION

Abraham Kuyper talked a lot about having a distinctly Christian worldview or, as he sometimes put it, "world and life view." For him this meant seeing all spheres of human life as directly under the rule of God. In family life, artistic activity, business, education, politics, and every other area, we must think about how God wants us to act in intentionally Christian ways.

Central to Kuyper's thinking about such matters was his conviction that God cares about the whole creation. In the beginning God looked at all of the things he had made and pronounced them to be good. When he created human beings, he placed them in the garden of Eden and commanded them to "rule over" the rest of his creation (Genesis 1:28). We humans are called to be caretakers in the world God has made. In Kuyper's school of thought, this obligation to take care of the creation and to cultivate it in God-obeying ways is referred to as the *cultural mandate.* The word "cultural" here doesn't refer just to things like appreciating opera and good literature. God's "rule over" command to Adam and Eve comes right after his telling them to "fill the earth," and this doesn't just mean they should have a lot of children—that was covered in the command right before that to "be fruitful and increase in number" (Genesis 1:28 again). What they were supposed to "fill" the earth with were the general products and patterns of human culture: language, labeling systems, tools, schedules, works of art, family activities. And all of these things were meant to glorify God.

Our first parents rebelled against God when they gave in to the serpent's challenge that they should try to be their own gods (Genesis 3). They decided to write their own rules and engage in all cultural activity in a way that would bring glory to themselves. This was a tragic turn of events. Their language was used to blaspheme. Their tools were used to murder (Cain and Abel in Genesis 4) and to try to build a tower that could reach heaven (the Babel project in Genesis 11). Their artistic skills were used to create idols. And much more.

But God did not give up, either on human beings or on the larger creation that he loves. He set out to call to himself a redeemed people who would show the world how he originally intended human beings to conduct their lives. And finally he sent Jesus to save individuals but also to reclaim the whole creation.

The people who are redeemed through the atoning work of Jesus are called by God to work at transforming culture—doing what they can here and now to honor God's original creating purposes for the world/cosmos. Of course, Kuyper was well aware that we cannot fully succeed in "Christianizing" the world. Sin continues to plague God's creation. The final transformation will come only when Jesus announces, "I am making everything new!" (Revelation 21:5).

A GOOD KIND OF "WORLDLINESS"

I talked to a group of Christian leaders recently about the ways in which we can represent the cause of the gospel in our public lives. I began by talking about the three different ways in which the biblical writers use the phrase "the world." The most familiar sense for many of us is the negative one, where "the world" refers to *the present sinful way of living.* When Jesus prayed for his disciples just before he went to the cross, he said that "the world has hated them, for they are not of the world any more than I am of the world" (John 17:14). And the apostle John warned his readers, "Do not love the world or anything in the world. If anyone loves the world, the love of the Father is not in him" (1 John 2:15). These passages clearly speak negatively about "the world."

Sometimes, though, "the world" has a neutral meaning, referring simply to a geographic expanse, *all the inhabited regions.* This is the meaning, for example, when Jesus says that "this gospel of the kingdom will be preached in the whole world" (Matthew 24:14).

The third meaning I talked about is a positive one. When the apostle John recorded Jesus' much-quoted words to Nicodemus, he used—for what our translations have as "the world"—the Greek word *kosmos,* which means *the whole created order:*

> For God so loved the *kosmos* that he gave his one and only Son, that whoever believes in him shall not perish but have eternal life. For God did not send his Son into the *kosmos* to condemn the *kosmos,* but to save the *kosmos* through him.
>
> *John 3:16–17*

This is the world, I explained, that God loves and wants to reclaim for his original creating purposes.

Several people came to me after my talk to tell me they had never before thought about this positive sense of "the world." The interesting thing is that these were not new Christians. Each of the folks who talked to me was a respected Christian leader doing significant things for the Christian cause. But they confessed to me that they had been pretty much stumbling along in their efforts to serve the Lord, sensing that they were involved in important things but not quite sure *why* what they were doing was important.

I see these folks as having been working with good Kuyperian instincts. They knew in their heart of hearts that God wanted them to serve him in the places where they spent their day-to-day lives. But the theology they were hearing in their churches and in other places where they were learning about the Christian life was not helping them understand the sense of calling they were experiencing in their hearts.

One of Kuyper's favorite phrases was "world and life view." He wanted Christian people to understand the world around them as created reality. And he wanted this understanding to make a difference in how they lived their everyday lives. That's exactly the kind of thing these folks I was talking to were looking for—a framework for serving the Lord on all the square inches on which they live and work as Christian disciples. That's the kind of "worldly" Christianity we need a lot more of!

GENTLENESS AND PATIENCE

Someone once told me that when I talk about Calvinism I sound like I'm "Abraham Kuyper on Prozac." I wasn't quite sure how he meant his comment, but I took it as a compliment. Kuyper was a very influential public leader, and he lived at a time in the Netherlands when Calvinism was still an important force in the larger society. Under those circumstances Kuyper could come across as quite triumphalist. When he talked about Christ ruling over every square inch of the creation, it is easy to imagine him thinking that he and his followers could quite legitimately go out and conquer many of those square inches in the name of Christ.

I do not entertain thoughts of that sort. In fact, I don't think it was healthy for Calvinists *ever* to have entertained those thoughts. The victory of the cause of the gospel over all the realities of sin will happen in God's own good time. The really big changes will happen when Christ returns. In the meantime we are called, not to win a lot of battles—not to conquer a lot of square inches—but to be faithful in the places where God has put us in response to the opportunities that God sends our way.

The important thing is to live in the assurance that the whole world does belong to God, that—as the hymn puts it—"though the wrong seems oft so strong, / God is the ruler yet." And this means that those of us who have been saved by sovereign grace have to bear witness to his sovereign rule over all things. When we go to school or work or play, we are going into his territory. All those square inches belong to him. And our task is to live as people who know the Ruler. It may not always be clear to us just how we are to acknowledge his ownership. But the question about how best to do so should always be on our minds. If this means we must act like "Abraham Kuyper on Prozac"— exhibiting a gentler and more patient Calvinism—so be it. But I prefer to think of it as living in a way that pleases a God who is himself gentle and patient.

chapter 8

THE GENEROSITY OPTION

once heard an interesting lecture by the Japanese theologian Kosuke Koyama. He made a point that especially stuck with me. We have to decide, he said, whether our theology is based on the idea of "a stingy God" or "a generous God."

Professor Koyama's comment made me do a lot of thinking. It struck me that Calvinism is often portrayed as believing in a God who is rather stingy with his saving grace. This was confirmed for me recently as I read some writers who are rather harsh in their criticisms of Calvinist thought. I was struck by how often they referred to the Calvinist God as rather stingy in dispensing his saving mercies.

A "SELECT FEW"?

A good sampling of this sort of portrayal can be found in a recent book by Dave Hunt, whose title alone gives a pretty good picture of his assessment of Calvinist theology: *What Love Is This? Calvinism's Misrepresentation of God.*[43] Over and over again, when describing or discussing the Calvinist view of election, Hunt uses the phrase "a select few." Here are a few examples:

- If lost sinners suffer from such an inability that they can be saved only by God's sovereign act of regeneration (and all men are not saved), it follows that God limits His mercy and grace to a *select few* [page 99, his italics].

- Why does the Holy Spirit through Scripture give the impression that God desires all men to repent while at the same time He withholds from all but a select few the essential means of repenting? [page 109].

- Why must God's infinite mercy be limited to a select few? [page 111].

- Sadly, the insistence that only a select few have been elected to salvation is not "good tidings of great joy to all people"! [page 414].

There can be no question that, in depicting the Calvinist God as favoring only "a select few," Hunt is correctly representing the views of many Calvinists. The idea of election has often been wedded to a belief in a remnant, a faithful minority—tied to a sense that God has bypassed the vast majority of the human race and bestowed his saving mercies on only a small number. Often this perspective seems to be worn as a badge of honor—as though Calvinists have a right to take pride in the fact that God has chosen them over most other members of the human race!

In thinking about this issue, though, we should at least be clear about a point of logic. In one of the remarks I just quoted from Dave Hunt, he gives the clear impression that, since Calvinists believe that people "can be saved only by God's act of regeneration," and if we also believe, as Calvinists do, that "all men are not saved," then we are *forced* to conclude that salvation is limited to the "select few." But, of course, there is an alternative. If you believe that not everyone will be saved, you could still hold that *more* than "a select few" will be saved by sovereign grace alone.

I need to make it clear once again that I am not a Universalist. Universalism holds that in the end everyone will be saved, and I reject that viewpoint. I believe that there will be a Last Judgment and that everyone who has refused God's offer of salvation in Jesus will be in huge trouble. The Scriptures seem to me to make it quite clear that those who stand in persistent opposition to God's redeeming purposes will find no place in the eternal kingdom.

At the same time, though, as I've gotten older I've found it increasingly difficult to draw sharp lines in my own mind about who is "in" and who is "out." And this, too, I get from the Bible. God alone will judge the human heart in the end. He works in mysterious ways. It seems to me that anyone who believes strongly in God's sovereignty is going to live with a lot of mystery on this subject.

THE BIBLE'S "NUMBERS GAME"

I have to admit there are some passages in the Bible that seem to come down on the side of divine stinginess. But none of these passages strike me as decisive in figuring out the way the Bible treats the "numbers game." The fact is that some of the passages sometimes quoted by Calvinists to support the "select few" notion don't really apply directly to the question of how many people will be saved in the end.

For example, Calvinists have sometimes defended the idea of a highly selective divine graciousness by quoting the speech Jesus made to the folks in his hometown of Nazareth:

> I assure you that there were many widows in Israel in Elijah's
> time. . . . Yet Elijah was not sent to any of them, but to a widow in
> Zarephath in the region of Sidon. And there were many in Israel with
> leprosy in the time of Elisha the prophet, yet not one of them was
> cleansed—only Naaman the Syrian.
>
> *Luke 4:25–27*

This certainly reinforces the idea of some sort of selectivity, but not necessarily a selectivity as to who will be *saved*. When Jesus had come to his hometown, the folks there demanded that he demonstrate the kind of power they had heard about from people in other towns. They knew him as the son of Joseph, so they felt they deserved some special evidence of his abilities. In this response, Jesus points to the example of prophets who had had plenty of opportunities to work miracles among their fellow Israelites but who instead were sent by God to single individuals in other territories. Jesus was saying, in effect, "Don't expect any special attention from me simply because I grew up in your midst."

Others have made much of the fact that Jesus says to his followers, "Do not be afraid, little flock, for your Father has been pleased to give you the kingdom" (Luke 12:32). This clearly implies, they argue, that the blessings of God's kingdom are meant for only a very small group. But the fact is that Jesus *is* literally talking here to a *very* small group, namely, the specially selected band of disciples he is sending out on an important mission—a missionary team to whom he also issues the very demanding requirement, "Sell your possessions and give to the poor" (12:33). There is no reason to think that he did not expect this missionary endeavor to result in the enlisting of other followers—thus adding perhaps many new members to the original "little flock."

One passage that does suggest smallness is Matthew 7:13–14, where Jesus describes the broad road that leads to destruction and the narrow road that leads in the direction of life, which "only a few find." As has often been noted,[44] however, this comes soon after Jesus, only a few verses before, offers the expansive promise that "everyone who asks receives; he who seeks finds; and to him who knocks, the door will be opened" (Matthew 7:8).

Without going into a detailed interpretation of specific texts, I will offer just this general observation: There is a genuine tension in the Scriptures between an emphasis on the difficulty of "getting in" and some strong indications that God's saving purposes are not confined to the categories we are inclined to construct. When someone asked the straightforward question of Jesus, "Lord, are only a few people going to be saved?" he did not give a numerical reply; he gave a command instead: "Make every effort to enter through the narrow door" (Luke 13:23–24). And John's great vision of the heavenly throng certainly gives us reason to expect that in the end there will be great numbers of people who have, in fact, found their way through the door:

> After this I looked and there before me was a great multitude that no one could count, from every nation, tribe, people and language, standing before the throne and in front of the Lamb. They were wearing white robes and were holding palm branches in their hands. And they cried out in a loud voice:
>
>> "Salvation belongs to our God,
>> who sits on the throne,
>> and to the Lamb."
>
> *Revelation 7:9–10*

HOPING FOR GENEROSITY

I do not know how to settle theological arguments about the "numbers game" in any decisive ways. If some Calvinists want to insist that only a very small portion of the human race will make it to heaven, I do not know how to convince them otherwise. But I hold out for divine generosity. And for me, this hope has to do with very specific cases.

Here is one: I have a rabbi friend who is now very old. He has often sent me friendly notes about something I have written, and on a number of occasions he has told me that he prays for God's blessing on my work. I have a spiritual hunch about how things are going to end up for this rabbi. I would not be surprised if, when the final encounter comes with his Maker and he sees the face of Jesus, he will bow in worship, acknowledging that Jesus is the One whom he should have named all along as the Promised One of Israel—*and* that the Savior will welcome him into the eternal kingdom.

Here is another case I have a strong hunch about: I know a woman who was abused by a father who was widely regarded as "a saint" in the Christian community. Her sense of violation by him runs so deep that she seems psychologically incapable of ever identifying with the Christian community. A few years ago, though, she acknowledged a long-standing problem with alcoholism and joined Alcoholics Anonymous. She told me that when she first started attending AA meetings, she could not bring herself to join the group in saying the Lord's Prayer, but now she does so—but, she quickly adds, only as a way of identifying with the group. When I think about what has happened to her, though, I see profound changes that look for all the world to me like the sorts of things that come from a conversion experience. So I wonder: Is it possible that in this process of surrendering her will to her "Higher Power," she has, at some level of her being, reached out to accept God's offer of salvation through Jesus Christ—even though she is at present psychologically incapable of articulating her experience in those terms?

Of course it's possible. But I am not sure about either her or the rabbi. Nor should I be. For one thing, I want to take very seriously what people say about what they believe. The woman in AA tells me she is not a Christian. And the rabbi is obviously a very devout Jew. Neither of them wants me to turn them into Christians without their permission. Furthermore, as a Christian who takes the Bible seriously, I do want them actually to call on the name of Jesus (Romans 10:13), to acknowledge that he alone can save them from their sinful state. In the meantime, however, I do live with my hunches about the scope of God's generosity toward people like them.

FINDING ENCOURAGEMENT FROM THE PAST

I don't feel I am betraying the Calvinist cause in entertaining these hunches. Indeed, I have found some encouragement on these matters from the Calvinist past. And my encouragers are not marginal to Calvinist history. Nineteenth-century Princeton Seminary is generally agreed to have been a bastion of solid Calvinist orthodoxy. The "Old Princeton" theologians who taught there saw themselves as chief defenders of, among other standards of "pure" Calvinism, the seventeenth-century Westminster Confession of Faith. So when I find some words of encouragement from both these Princeton thinkers and the Westminster Confession, I can be sure I have not wandered too far from the Calvinist path.

So first, an encouraging word from Old Princeton. This comes from A. A. Hodge, who succeeded his father, the great Charles Hodge, as a theology professor:

> Although heaven can only be entered by the holy, yet such, we are assured, is the infinite provision made for human salvation, and such the intense love for human sinners therein exhibited, that the multitude of the redeemed will be incomparably greater than the number of the lost. My father [Charles Hodge], at the close of his long life spent in the defense of Calvinism, wrote on one of his conference papers, in trembling characters, a little while before he died, "I am fully persuaded that the vast majority of the human race will share in the beatitudes and glories of our Lord's redemption." Remember that all who die before complete moral agency have been given to Christ. Remember that the vast populations of the coming millenniums are given to Christ. Then shall the promises of Christ to the great "father of the faithful" be fulfilled to the letter: "Thy seed shall be like the sands of the sea-shore."[45]

Obviously, it would be interesting to explore some of the theological hints that are thrown out in this statement. But quite apart from these technical matters, it is clear that there is an expansive spirit at work in these comments—a trust in divine generosity.

The second word of encouragement comes from a document not known for its expansive spirit. But I do find an encouraging word in what is actually just a passing reference in the Westminster Confession's brief discussion of "effectual calling," the Calvinist idea that when God sets out to save someone there is no possibility of failure. Having insisted that God uses "his Word and Spirit" to bring those he has predestined to eternal life out of their sinful state into a conscious understanding of the gospel, the Confession immediately introduces an exception to this pattern: "Elect infants, dying in infancy"—and thus not having arrived at a conscious understanding of the claims of the gospel, nonetheless—"are regenerated and saved by Christ through the Spirit, who worketh when, and where, and how he pleaseth."[46]

Again, this hardly exudes with a spirit of divine generosity. Most Christians are willing to say without qualification that all children who die in infancy are saved; but the Westminster writers refused to state it that way, limiting their generosity to "elect infants." This makes it all the more intriguing when they add this observation. Not only are elect infants "regenerated and saved by Christ through the Spirit, who worketh when, and where, and how he pleaseth"; but "So also are all other elect persons who are incapable of being outwardly called by the ministry of the Word."

Who are these non-infant people who are numbered among the elect, even though they are "incapable of being outwardly called by the ministry of the Word"? No explanation is given. All the Confession does is point to the possibility that some people are elected by God to eternal life, even though they are not in a position to hear the gospel proclaimed.

This certainly has application to those who live in places where the gospel has not been preached. But it can also be expanded, I think, to apply to people like my rabbi friend, who because of what he knows about a rather shameful history of Christian persecution of the Jews may not be capable of focusing clearly on the true person of Christ. And to a young woman who has been deeply wounded by the Christian community but who has found healing in another sort of community—one that encourages her to yield her life to a "Higher Power" and, having done so, to pray the prayer that Jesus taught to his disciples.

Again, I am not sure about all of this. But I do have my hunches and my hopes—and a few words of encouragement from solid Calvinists from the past. I also have a fundamental Calvinist conviction that looms large for me whenever I think about such matters: the clear biblical teaching that God is sovereign, that his ways are not our ways.

So here too I can only sing the hymn that Paul sings in Romans 11. In a book about a theology that emphasizes God's sovereignty it is surely permissible to sing it twice:

> Oh, the depth of the riches of the wisdom and knowledge of God!
>> How unsearchable his judgments,
>> and his paths beyond tracing out!
> "Who has known the mind of the Lord?
>> Or who has been his counselor?"
> "Who has ever given to God,
>> that God should repay him?"
> For from him and through him and to him are all things.
>> To him be the glory forever! Amen.
>
> *Romans 11:33–36*

chapter 9

SADNESS AND HOPE IN LAS VEGAS

am writing this shortly after returning home from Las Vegas. Actually, the point of going there this time was to hang around for a while in the airport, so I planned a Las Vegas stopover on a return trip from a speaking engagement. I arrived late in the evening, and, after a night's sleep at a nearby hotel, I put in several hours the next morning in the airport where the scene from *Hardcore* took place.

I had flown to Las Vegas from the Denver airport, and as I walked to my departure gate in Denver, I saw a middle-aged Orthodox Jewish man sitting alone. He was wearing what I have come to think of as the Orthodox uniform: black suit, open-collared white shirt, wide-brimmed black hat, full beard. I've often thought it would be interesting to interview such a person. Here are the sorts of questions I would ask: "What do you make of all this—all these other people who represent such different views of the world from your own? What is it like going from your own community, where everyone dresses like you, to a place like this, where you are obviously different from almost everyone else? Do you ever wish, someplace deep in your heart, that you could be like the rest of the people here? Is your sense of religious identity strengthened or weakened when you are in an airport?"

Now, in going to Las Vegas, I was going to pose those same kinds of questions to myself. I don't wear distinctive Calvinist clothes, but I do wear a spiritual "uniform" that is every bit as out of place in airports as the Orthodox Jew's literal garb. Jake Van Dorn had sat in the Las Vegas airport and talked to a relative stranger about Calvinism, and I must confess that I was embarrassed to listen to his conversation. Hearing him explain TULIP in that setting, using words I have often uttered in "home" settings to summarize what I believe—well, to be honest, it had made me cringe. And I know it wasn't because Jake was a caricature. I know too many real-life Jakes. I know *myself* too well.

So I had decided to put myself to the test. I would hang around the Las Vegas airport while concentrating on my Calvinist "uniform," and I would observe other people carefully, taking a kind of spiritual inventory—trying to identify the deeper impulses and yearnings—of what I might see and hear.

THINKING ABOUT LAS VEGAS

Actually, this wasn't the first time I had thought about the spiritual meaning of what goes on in Las Vegas. Several years ago I offered some reflections on the city in a short book I wrote about popular culture.[47] I was motivated to do so after reading a newspaper feature by a bored journalist who had decided to justify a weekend trip to Las Vegas by writing a snide first-person piece about some of the things that especially offended his aesthetic sensibilities. I only wrote a few pages on the subject, but I did note that Las Vegas is an easy target for the barbs of its cultured despisers. Is there any way of saying an interesting theological word about this city that seems to be a supreme example of bad taste?

Las Vegas certainly struck me as fair game for theological critique. Indeed, it seems to be despised by thinkers across the theological spectrum. Christian conservatives hate Las Vegas because of its gambling, booze, and promiscuity; liberals because of its greed, bad taste, and sexism.

In that earlier reflection I was especially interested in something the journalist had said, something I had heard before but whose theological significance had hit me now for the first time. Once you are inside a Las Vegas hotel-casino complex, the reporter wrote, you lose all sense of time; it is difficult to know, for example, whether it is early afternoon or the middle of the night.

When I read his comment, I remembered a few lines from a hymn we had sung in my childhood:

> In the land of fadeless day
> lies the city foursquare;
> it shall never pass away
> and there is no night there.

That hymn was based on the Bible's portrayal in the book of Revelation of the new Jerusalem. And this is what struck me as theologically interesting: some of the things people mention when they talk about Las Vegas are also things the Bible says about the "new Jerusalem"—which in its own way is also a glittering, opulent, bustling center of never-ending festivity (see Revelation 21 and 22).

This matchup should not surprise us, I argued. Las Vegas may be a very wicked city, but it is precisely in its wickedness that it is also a significant spiritual environment. People go to Las Vegas with deep yearnings for security and satisfaction. It is a place that symbolizes promise. Its psychic currency is the stuff of which our dreams are made. Here is a case where popular, glitzy culture reveals some important things about the human quest.

EAVESDROPPING

The "Las Vegas never sleeps" theme was confirmed in my brief van ride in the morning from my hotel to the airport. The driver was mainly interested in talking to my fellow passengers, two young women who were heading home to Philadelphia. "Did you have a good time?" he asked them. "Oh, yeah," one of them responded. "We haven't slept for four days." "We haven't even had time to *think*," her friend added.

My earlier visits to Las Vegas had been on stopovers on driving trips, so this was my first time in the airport. It had been fairly quiet when I arrived at night, but in the morning it was bustling. There were large crowds and long lines—all supplemented by the action at the omnipresent slot machines.

My sense that Las Vegas is a city of spiritual contradictions was reinforced by two signs in front of the Prickly Pear airport restaurant. One sign had huge letters: ALL DAY BREAKFAST. Only four feet away was a second sign in small letters: NOW SERVING BREAKFAST UNTIL 10:30 A.M. It was only 9:00 a.m., so I went in and ordered the omelet special.

As I ate, I was positioned between two couples, and I tried to listen to both conversations. One was deeply engaged in a discussion of problems in their synagogue back home. The husband was telling his wife that the lay leader of the temple council, Elliot, wasn't very happy about the way the rabbi was making some of the decisions about programs. The husband was on Elliot's side, but the wife thought they should all "give the rabbi some space."

The second couple were African-Americans, and they seemed to be from New York City. As he read the *New York Times,* he offered a running commentary about Mayor Bloomberg's performance. He did not like the mayor, and his wife seemed to be agreeing with his negative assessment.

Both conversations focused on leadership. It was interesting to hear them talk, but I heard nothing I could not have encountered in any other airport. And maybe that was a good point to ponder. Maybe for many folks Las Vegas is a momentary distraction. The two young women in the van would go home to get some sleep, and then they'd go back to their ordinary routines. And the two couples would return to the kinds of things we all worry about from day to day—in their cases, rather normal concerns about people whom they wish were doing a better job of leading in the areas that affect their lives.

TWO GRANDMOTHERS

Once on the plane, though, I ran into some strong feelings about Las Vegas. I had just settled into my aisle seat in the coach section when a family of three—a young married couple and an older woman—came to my row. They asked, in heavily accented English, if I would mind moving across the aisle so that the three of them could sit together. I agreed. They were profuse in their expressions of gratitude.

I enjoy air travel. I appreciate the opportunity to read or to watch a movie. What I do *not* like to do is talk to other passengers. This time, however, I felt an obligation to continue my theological research, and I took the goodwill of the three passengers across the aisle to be offering the opportunity I needed. I asked the young man how long they had been in Las Vegas. "For the long weekend," he answered. "Did you have a good time?" I asked. "Some of it, yes. But we are also sad," he replied. "My mother-in-law is the gambler, and she lost much money."

His mother-in-law leaned over and told me that, to be exact, she had lost six thousand dollars. "So that is why we are sad," she said. "But soon we will be happy." She gently patted her pregnant daughter's tummy area. "Very soon I will be a grandmother again!" At that, the young couple grinned sheepishly.

I asked my three fellow passengers where they were from. "We live now in Los Angeles," said the young man. "But ten years ago we came from Azerbaijan." After a brief pause, he added, "It is much better here." Then an even briefer pause: "Except when we come to Las Vegas and lose much money gambling."

His mother-in-law seemed eager to redirect the conversation. "Where are *you* from?" she asked me. I told her that I also live in the Los Angeles area. "No," she shot back, "*before* that!" I told her I was born in New Jersey. And then she tried again: "No, before *that*. Where was your grandmother from?"

I know almost nothing about my father's mother, who died when he was a child, so I answered about my maternal grandmother, whom I knew well. I told the Azerbaijani woman that my grandmother came from the Netherlands. She smiled and sat back.

If I had been able to continue the conversation, trying to explain my Calvinist convictions to the woman who asked about my origins, I would have stayed with the topic of my grandmother and what she brought with her from her village in the Netherlands.

As I calculate distances, the Dutch village where my grandmother was born is about 5400 miles from Las Vegas. When her family sailed the seas to make a new home in New Jersey, she covered a good portion of that 5400-mile distance. But her family brought their Calvinism with them, and it seemed to travel well. Now, more than a century later, I was bringing it the rest of the way to Las Vegas.

I don't sense that my grandmother's Calvinist perspective has lost its durability in the wear and tear of travel and time. To be sure, it now has to be put to some new uses, answering some new questions, facing some new challenges. And I know I have reshaped it a bit into a kinder and gentler Calvinism. But in its new settings—even in the Las Vegas airport—it retains for me the basic marks of the sturdy village faith that it once had been.

MEMORIZING A COMFORTING ANSWER

In February of 1626, the Church of England sponsored a series of conferences where the disagreements between Calvinists and Arminians were debated. Representatives of the Anglican Church had participated in the Synod of Dordrecht in 1618–1619, which had produced the famed Canons of Dordt. This involvement had reinforced the hope of many English Puritans that the Calvinist perspective might become the official position of the Church of England. Indeed, toward the end of the last of these conference debates, the Puritan party proposed that "the Synod of Dordt [be] ... established here by authority in the Church of England." The historian Irvonwy Morgan tells us that at this point in the meeting Francis White, a leader of the anti-Calvinists, quickly jumped to his feet and addressed the officials presiding over the session with this anguished plea: "I beseech your Lordships that we of the Church of England be not put to borrow a new faith from any village in the Netherlands."[48]

The religion that my grandmother's family brought with them to America was very much a Dutch village faith. They emigrated in the 1880s from Sliedrecht, a village only about five miles from the larger town of Dordrecht. I never heard my grandmother talk about technical points of doctrine, but Calvinism was the only theology she ever knew. Her father, my great-grandfather, lived into his nineties. By the time I came along he was long retired from his factory job. What I remembered about him is that he smoked cigars and read his Dutch Bible with a magnifying glass. And he did like to talk about theology.

While I'm sure my great-grandfather could have given a good explanation of the TULIP doctrines, I doubt my grandmother could have done so. But I have no doubt that she could have quoted from memory the First Question and Answer of the Heidelberg Catechism, often referred to simply as "Heidelberg One":

Q: What is thy only comfort in life and death?

A: That I with body and soul, both in life and death, am not my own, but belong unto my faithful Savior Jesus Christ; who, with his precious blood, hath fully satisfied for all my sins, and delivered me from all the power of the devil; and so preserves me that without the will of my heavenly Father, not a hair can fall from my head; yea, that all things must be subservient to my salvation, and therefore, by his Holy Spirit, he also assures me of eternal life, and makes me sincerely willing and ready, henceforth to live unto him.

Every Dutch Calvinist child learned that question and answer. And there are many stories of old folks who would quote Heidelberg One with their dying breaths.

Life in urban New Jersey was very different for my grandmother's family from what it had been in their Dutch village. But for them Heidelberg One traveled well. And it still travels well for me. And it continues to do so for the next generations in my family. My son and daughter-in-law taught Heidelberg One to their two boys, one six and the other three, who now have it memorized.

HOPE EVEN IN LOSS AND SADNESS

There were no visible clues about the religious affiliation, if any, of the Azerbaijani family on the plane. I know a little about Azerbaijan's religious traditions—predominantly Muslim, with much Orthodox influence as well. Azerbaijan is also the birthplace of Zoroaster and the religion that bears his name. If I could have had a relaxed conversation with this family, I would have asked them about their background. It may have been an interesting path to pursue with them. But I already had plenty to work with. They had told me about loss and sadness. They had also expressed hope for the future, focusing on a baby that would soon be born.

Indeed, my grandmother could have found much in common with their experiences. She too had traveled a long distance to settle in America. She understood loss and sadness—I'll never forget the bitterness she expressed when she told me, not long before she died, about the night one of her children, a teenage son, lay dying of a burst appendix as she waited for a doctor who never responded to their urgent calls to come.

But she also knew about hope. And for her as well, hope focused on the birth of a baby. But this was the baby she heard about in her Calvinist church, the baby whose birth at Bethlehem we sing about at

Christmas: "the hopes and fears of all the years / are met in thee tonight."

My grandmother would have understood the basic hopes and fears at work in the lives of the Azerbaijani travelers. I think she would have seen clearly the connection between the concerns they were struggling with and a very important question lurking just beneath the surface of their conscious lives: "What is your only comfort in life and death?"

ILLUSIONS

I came away from this visit to Las Vegas with my Calvinism intact— including my belief in human depravity, particularly my own depravity. I have to confess that I feel the lure of Las Vegas within my own soul. Las Vegas calls to me when I look down on its glittering lights from a plane window on a late flight home, or when I catch my first glimpse of it rising up out of the desert as we approach it by car on a trip east. It called to me again this time as I walked around the airport. I sensed not just its superficial temptations but some of its deeper spiritual impulses as well.

This is to be expected. Las Vegas is a counterfeit version of the "new Jerusalem," and it shares something of the glorious reality it mocks. But it cannot really chase the night away or put an end to our sorrows. It calls to us, but it does not deliver on its promises. No genuine security or satisfaction is to be found within its dazzling casino walls. It does not quiet the profound restlessness of our hearts.

My wife and I once stayed in Las Vegas on the first night of a vacation trip, as we drove by car to Idaho. We spent an hour or so on a walking tour. Entering one casino, we came upon a family in turmoil. The father had just discovered that his wallet was missing. A look of horror came over him, and suddenly he began to run. His wife screamed after him hysterically; the two children, one a teenager, began to cry. In their frantic sobbings I heard a deep desperation. Las

Vegas had offered them a counterfeit vision of human fulfillment, luring them with the false promise that the good life is made possible primarily by the kinds of things we can carry around in our wallets.

As we walked away from this sad scene, I looked up and saw a sign bearing the name of one of Las Vegas's establishments—"The Mirage."

chapter 10

JAKE'S MISTAKE

There is no question in my mind that Jake's *Hardcore* conversation with Niki was a disaster. You don't respond to Niki's curiosity about religion with a mini-lecture about TULIP. But how *do* you respond? What would a more adequate version of the conversation look like? Would it have to be put in very contemporary terms? And would even that answer soon become outdated, so that a century later the right sort of answer would be different yet again?

I spend a lot of my time with people who study new methods for communicating the gospel. They are tuned in to the different ways in which various age groups—Boomers, Gen-Xers, Millennials, and so on—understand things. I have learned some good things from these folks. But on the question of what Jake should have said to Niki, I am not ready simply to turn the problem over to them for a solution. On this one, I have my own hunch, and it is a strong one. I think Jake's mistake was not that he reached into the past for a way of explaining things to Niki; it's just that in reaching into the past he grabbed the wrong thing.

Jake went to the right period of history for his response. But he went to the wrong city. He should have reached back to sixteenth-century Heidelberg rather than to seventeenth-century Dordrecht. I wish that, instead of talking about Dordt's TULIP doctrines, Jake had spoken in very personal terms to Niki about the First Question and Answer of the Heidelberg Catechism.

COMPARING QUESTIONS AND ANSWERS

I once heard the Dutch theologian Hendrikus Berkhof compare the opening questions of each of the two great catechisms of the Calvinist tradition, the Heidelberger, which came from Germany, and the Westminster Shorter Catechism, which was produced by Scottish Presbyterians. Berkhof explained that, while the two catechisms generally contain the same Calvinist content, they differ greatly in their tone. This is obvious, he said, in the way each of them begins. The first question of the Westminster Shorter Catechism makes a rather abstract theological point, talking about "man"—humankind—in general: "What is the chief end of man?" it asks, then giving this well-known answer: "Man's chief end is to glorify God, and to enjoy him forever." But the Heidelberg Catechism, said Berkhof, begins in very personal terms: "What is *your* only comfort in life and death?" And the answer: "That *I* with body and soul, both in life and death, am not *my* own, but belong to *my* faithful Savior Jesus Christ."

Both questions, with their corresponding answers, are important. But Professor Berkhof pointed out that there is something very contemporary-sounding in the tone of the Heidelberger. This is how he put it: Heidelberg One asks us to speak, he said, *existentially.* It addresses us, not as "man" in general, but as flesh-and-blood individuals in the midst of the day-to-day realities of our lives. "What is *your* only comfort?" "That *I* am not my own." "That *I* belong."

Professor Berkhof gave that lecture—a memorable one for me—in the early 1960s during a visit to the United States. His use of "existential" to describe the tone of Heidelberg One had a nice feel to it then—the philosophy of existentialism was quite popular at the time. That term, along with the philosophical movement with which it was associated, is not as prominent these days. But the idea behind the term still captures the mood of much of our culture. One of the motifs, for example, that is often associated these days with the postmodern way of viewing things is the notion of "personal narrative." People find it important to "tell their story." If we are to get beyond purely personal concerns, they are convinced, it will have to be because our individual stories somehow intersect with other stories. The personal-story theme also looms large in Christian circles, where many theologians these days emphasize the importance of religious "narrative" as over against "abstract propositions" about God and his purposes.

I have to confess that I still like the abstractions. But I do have to admit that they don't play the same role in my life as the very personal statements about what God and his purposes mean *for me*. Heidelberg One, then, not only gets at something that is central to my Calvinist faith; it also seems to connect nicely to a widespread contemporary mood.

MISSING CONNECTIONS

Not that Heidelberg One is restricted to questions about very personal matters. Actually, my first real inkling that Calvinism might have some connection to issues of social justice issues happened when I heard someone quote Heidelberg One. I was a young seminarian, and I was sent on a preaching assignment to a congregation in a Dutch-American community in a neighboring state. I arrived on Saturday and was an overnight guest in the home of a church elder and his wife. After dinner that evening the husband read—as was the custom in that subculture—a chapter from the Scriptures. I don't remember the passage, but I do know that when he finished reading, he told me that the verses reminded him of Heidelberg One, adding that it is wonderful for a person to be able to say, "My only comfort in life and death is that I am not my own."

We soon left the table and sat in the living room, where he turned on the evening news. The main news story was about Martin Luther King leading a march against housing discrimination. My host grew agitated, and he walked over to turn off the TV set, telling me he couldn't stand to hear "all of this stuff about the colored people and their complaints." I immediately let him know that my sympathies were with Dr. King, and we soon were engaged in a heated argument. At one point he pounded his fist on the coffee table and shouted, "I don't want those people moving into my neighborhood! What I have I got on my own, and no one is going to take it away from me!"

I realized it was pointless to keep the argument going, and things soon calmed down. Later, when I lay in bed, the irony hit me: the person who had shouted that what he possessed he had gotten on his own and no one could take it away from him had only minutes before told me that his only comfort in life and death was that he was not his own. That lesson stayed with me. Furthermore, I came to see that the concluding words of the answer to Question One contain all the basics necessary for a Calvinist activism: God's Spirit "makes me sincerely willing and ready, henceforth to live unto him."

Heidelberg One traveled well for me, both in my own very personal life and in the more corporate dimensions of my faith.

AN "EXISTENTIAL" CONVERSATION IN THE AIRPORT

So now, back to Jake and his conversation with Niki in the Las Vegas airport. Again, Jake took the wrong approach. He should have talked about Heidelberg One rather than TULIP. He should have begun with the "existential."

Frankly, I'm not sure TULIP is ever a good topic for casual conversations with people who are not Calvinists. TULIP works best as a "looking back" framework. A person has experienced the grace of God in a marvelous way in her life and she wants to look back and think about how it all happened. The TULIP doctrines are a summary—the right one, as I view things—of the way God goes about saving people. But TULIP is not something that is designed to attract a person to

Christianity in the first place. If Jake had been seriously interested in inviting Niki into the kind of faith he had experienced, talking about TULIP was the wrong approach.

But I suspect what was really misguided was the fact that Jake engaged in the wrong kind of conversation. Niki had asked him about his religious perspective—and he decided to give her a brief theology lesson. Once he got "the truth" out, he was content to bring the conversation to a close. He was not at all surprised that his views were not attractive to her. He was content to dismiss the subject in this way: "I admit it's a little confusing when you look at it from the outside. You have to try to look at it from the inside."

As I said when I first reported this conversation, I wish Jake had taken a different tack in his dialogue with Niki. I wish he would have started out by showing an interest in how *she* viewed things from "inside" *her* view of life. He might have picked up, for example, on her comment that she was a "Venusian." What did she mean? I did a Google search on that word and found nothing that was helpful. But I do know about Titian's painting, "Festival of Love," which features the worship of Venus, the goddess of love. The painting depicts many cupids, themselves the offspring of Venus's various love affairs, dedicating themselves to promoting sexual passion. My guess is that Niki shared that general outlook on life.

Incidentally, Titian painted this "Venusian" scene during the years 1518 to 1520. It was the sixteenth century, the time when Calvinism was being born. In fact, he painted it exactly a hundred years before the period (1618–1619) when the Synod of Dordt was in session. There might be material to work with there in imagining a further conversation between Niki and Jake. At the very least, this is not simply the case of a person with an older way of viewing things encountering someone with a relatively new perspective. Properly understood, the two of them represent worldviews that have existed side by side for several centuries.

A COMPASSIONATE APPROACH THAT LISTENS FOR NIKI'S STORY

I was talking in class one day about the need to reach out to non-Christians "where they are"—attempting to understand their cultural context, their present worldview, their individual life circumstances. This is what is known as a "relational evangelism" approach. We engage others with empathy, and we hope to gain the credibility to talk to them about the basic issues of life.

A student came up to me after my lecture. "I think you make it too complicated," he said. "We just need to tell people they are sinners and then hope that the Holy Spirit will use this to convict them of their sin." This is a very common approach in the evangelical world, and it fits nicely with a rather harsh version of Calvinism. But it is not my brand of Calvinism.

I think it would have been important, for example, for Jake not simply to condemn the *content* of Niki's worldview and its accompanying lifestyle. He would do well to find out some things about her own personal story. In the light of the studies of young women who get into the way of thinking and acting typified by Niki, it is not unreasonable to suspect that there was some sort of abuse in her background. Perhaps she has gotten into a pattern of behavior—dominated by drugs and promiscuous sex—that stems from an inability to accept genuine love from another person. Maybe she has learned that the best way to make it through life is to manipulate others, especially men. And maybe all this is rooted in a fundamental inability to *trust*.

If anything like this is true of Niki's story, then the worst thing for a Calvinist to do would be to begin by telling her she is a horrible sinner who must repent and straighten out her ways. And that *would* be the message conveyed by beginning with TULIP, which could easily send her the message that she is a horrible person who may already have been rejected by God from the very foundations of the world.

To be sure, her patterns of behavior *are* grounded in her rebellion against the living God. But in this case that rebellion has produced a life in which there is much loneliness and pain. Rather than going straight to the rebellion, it is a good thing to identify the loneliness and pain in the deep places of her life. Instead of hitting Niki directly with the "high Calvinism" of the TULIP doctrines, I would rather have her hear a compassionate word. Charles Spurgeon put the general point here well:

> We win hearts for Jesus by love, by sympathy with their sorrows, by anxiety lest they should perish, by pleading with God for them with all our hearts that they would not be left to die unsaved, by pleading with them for God, that, for their own sake, they would seek mercy and find grace.[49]

If I'm right about Niki, she did not need a theology lesson. She needed a God who spoke to her in soft and tender tones. She needed to hear about the possibility of belonging to a Savior who would not "own" her in an enslaving way but as a divine Lover who would never abandon her—whose unfailing faithfulness would be her only comfort in life or in death.

This is what Jake should have talked about with Niki. And the TULIP doctrines, if they were to come into the picture at all for Niki, could be dealt with much further down the line.

chapter 11

CONFESSIONS OF A
TRAVELING CALVINIST

y main hope for Niki, if I ever had a chance to talk with her, would be that she come to put her trust in Jesus Christ. If she eventually accepted the Calvinist way of viewing things, I would also be immensely pleased. But I wouldn't feel horrible if that did not happen. Maybe, after hearing the message about Jesus and coming to trust in him as her Savior, she would join a local Assembly of God. Or a Methodist congregation. Or maybe she would even become a devout Roman Catholic. I want to say this clearly: that would be okay with me as a Calvinist.

WHO WOULD YOU WANT TO TALK TO HER?

I once proposed an interesting little exercise to a small group of evangelical Christians. I asked them to think of a young woman they cared deeply about but who was not a Christian. Suppose you could make it happen that this young woman would spend several days of relaxed time with a well-known Christian leader who would talk with her about her relationship with God. Whom would you choose from the list I'm giving you? Then I gave them evangelical names they were familiar with, all either television evangelists or prominent theologians.

But I also included two Roman Catholics—the priest Henri Nouwen and Mother Teresa (both of whom were alive at the time). I wasn't surprised at their choices. They all chose one of the two Catholics.

This experiment demonstrated two things to all of us: first, that our evangelical attitudes toward Roman Catholicism had changed significantly in recent years, and second, that when it comes down to someone we love dearly who is not a Christian, what many of us care about most is that they see living examples of what it means to have a warm, trusting relationship with Jesus. The evangelists and theologians I put on the list were respected as folks who might have articulated the right verbal message, but the group did not see them as folks who would effectively communicate the love of Jesus to the young woman. For this the group looked to people like Nouwen and Mother Teresa (and, I am sure, Billy Graham, if I had included him as a candidate).

I have a strong suspicion that my grandmother would not approve of my thoughts and sentiments on this point. Here I simply have to say that her experience was rather limited. I love to return in my spirit to the villages of my ancestors, and I want to remain loyal to their basic theological convictions. But I have had to rework their theology in the light of what I experience as a Christian who is forced to think ecumenically and globally on a daily basis. I have learned too much from the inhabitants of other villages to ever fit neatly into their Dutch village life. I have been taught by the residents of monasteries and convents, slums in Mexico City, black townships in South Africa, Jewish ghettos in Eastern Europe, Amish farming settlements in Manitoba, and refugee camps in the Middle East. So while Sliedrecht and Dordrecht continue to be spiritual landmarks for me when I return there for spiritual and theological nurture, I know I carry lessons and loyalties with me that would not have pleased either my grandmother or the learned churchmen who gathered at the seventeenth-century Synod of Dordt.

"NEARLY PERFECT" CHRISTIANITY?

Recently I read a book about Calvinism written in the 1920s. The author, R. B. Kuiper, was an old-fashioned Calvinist who liked to set forth rather bold claims on behalf of the system of thought he was defending. "Calvinism," he wrote, "is the most nearly perfect interpretation of Christianity. In the final analysis Calvinism and Christianity are practically synonymous." And to reinforce his point he quoted a similar sentiment from the great nineteenth-century Princeton theologian Benjamin Warfield: "Calvinism is just religion in its purity. We have only, therefore, to conceive of religion in its purity, and that is Calvinism."[50]

I have to admit that when I read remarks of this sort on behalf of Calvinism, I usually cringe a little. They strike me as claiming too much on Calvinism's behalf. But in this case my reaction was not so negative, because two pages earlier R. B. Kuiper had set the stage for his seemingly bold claims with a more modest statement. Even "the most ardent Calvinist," he wrote, "can hardly maintain that his interpretation of the Christian religion is perfectly full-orbed, and that no other interpretation contains aught to supplement it."[51]

In what sense, then, did the author believe that Calvinism is the "nearly perfect" interpretation of Christianity? Well, not in the sense that only Calvinists are true Christians. He was making a much more charitable point, namely, that all true Christians are, whether they know it or not, Calvinists at heart. A person, he says, "may not call himself a Calvinist; he may even resent being called by this name"— but that's what he is "in the final analysis" if he "lives in utter dependence upon God."[52]

This is not unlike the view of Calvinism that Charles Spurgeon endorsed when he said, in a remark I quoted earlier, that if anyone would ask him what he means when he calls himself a Calvinist, he would respond that a Calvinist is someone who says, *Salvation is of the Lord.* In saying this, Spurgeon was not insisting that only a Calvinist truly believes that salvation can only come from a sovereign God. He was expressing a confidence that everyone—whatever the theological system to which a person explicitly subscribes—who genuinely experiences a total dependence on divine mercy for their salvation is a Calvinist in spirit.

I have much sympathy for this way of putting it. But I am still reluctant to say this kind of thing myself. For one thing, it seems a bit condescending. The Jesuit theologian Karl Rahner once argued that there are people in non-Christian religions who are "anonymous Christians."[53] By this he meant that some Muslims or Hindus might actually be motivated by a genuine Christlike spirit, even though they would never claim to adhere to uniquely Christian teachings. But this way of stating the case did not always go over well with scholars representing other religious traditions. They complained that the "anonymous Christian" label was an expression of Christian arrogance; they wanted to be taken seriously for what they actually said they believed *as* Hindus or Muslims. I have the same sense about proclaiming my Methodist or Catholic friends to be "anonymous Calvinists."

But I also think that designating all true Christians as Calvinists claims more for Calvinism than we have a right to claim. I am firmly convinced that Calvinism is right about some extremely important matters of faith. I am not prepared, however, to say with Warfield that "Calvinism is just religion in its purity"—mainly because I don't think that Calvinism really does justice to many dimensions of Christian discipleship.

AN EMBARRASSING WEAKNESS

One area, for example, where I believe Calvinism has been embarrassingly weak is in ethics—an important part of the Christian life for any perspective that claims to be, in Warfield's words, "religion in its purity." Calvinists have certainly not stood out in the Christian community as especially pure people when it comes to the way they behave. They have frequently been intolerant, sometimes to the point of taking abusive and violent action toward people with whom they have disagreed. They have often promoted racist policies. And the fact that they have often defended these things by appealing directly to Calvinist teachings suggests that at least something in these patterns may be due to some weaknesses in the Calvinist perspective itself. On such matters, it seems clear to me that Calvinists ought to repent and admit to the larger Christian community that we have much to learn from others—from Mennonites, from black members of South African Pentecostal churches, from the followers of Saint Francis, and many others.

If nowhere else, then at least on ethical matters, Calvinists could stand to develop considerable humility. John Calvin himself lifted up humility as a central virtue. He makes this observation:

> A saying of Chrysostom's has always pleased me very much, that the foundation of our philosophy is humility. But that of Augustine pleases me even more: "When a certain rhetorician was asked what was the chief rule in eloquence, he replied, 'Delivery'; what was the second rule, 'Delivery'; what was the third rule, 'Delivery'; so if you ask me concerning the precepts of the Christian religion, first, second, third, and always I would answer, 'Humility.'"[54]

Humility is an important virtue to cultivate in dealing with the basic issues of the Christian life. And when it comes to ethical issues, Calvinists do well to cultivate this virtue in large doses.

A DESIRE TO LEARN FROM OTHERS

But, of course, humility by itself is not enough. After all, a group of people could decide to be humble about the fact that they alone possess the truth about the basic issues of life! This sort of humility can at best produce an attitude of tolerance toward all the other misguided souls in the world. I prefer a theological humility that is coupled with a genuine desire to *learn from others*.

I have learned so much from other Christian traditions that I have come to think of myself as an *eclectic* Calvinist. I draw freely from other traditions in fleshing out my theology. I do not see my Calvinism as locking me into a closed system of thought that must resist at all costs any outside theological influences.

And this should be expected, because Calvinism as such cannot survive as a closed system. "Mere Calvinism," as summarized in the TULIP doctrines, does not cover a wide enough theological territory to serve in this way. As I argued earlier, the TULIP doctrines address the fundamentally important question of how an individual gets right with God. But the answer to this question—of which TULIP is a summary—does not a whole theology make.

"Mere Calvinism" *needs* fleshing out—and Calvinists have done so in many different ways. If you were to gather together a cross section of people who enthusiastically agree with each other about TULIP, you would find that they nonetheless disagree on a number of other important theological questions. Anglican Calvinists' doctrine of the church differs from that of Congregational Calvinists. Baptist and Reformed Calvinists argue about adult baptism versus infant baptism. And even within each of these groups people debate questions about the proper methods of evangelism, the best way to understand the Lord's Supper, questions about ordination, how best to relate to the larger culture, and so on. Once we get beyond the TULIP doctrines, then, Calvinism itself is a theologically diverse movement.

But when I admit to being eclectic, I am making more than the obvious point—that "mere Calvinism" does not by itself give us a doctrine of the church, the sacraments, and so on. I don't just learn from Calvinists who have fleshed out the TULIP doctrines in different ways. I have found it helpful, even necessary, to learn from theological perspectives that pose alternative answers to those of the TULIP doctrines themselves.

LEARNING FROM DIVERSITY

Someone once asked me, "How can a Calvinist like you survive—especially as the president!—at a school as diverse as Fuller Theological Seminary?" I wish I would have asked her which part she found most puzzling: that I could tolerate Fuller's diversity, or that Fuller could tolerate my Calvinism!

For my part, I have to say that I thrive on the interaction. You don't hang around at a place like Fuller Seminary simply to keep your theological perspective intact; for that you're better off looking for another place to hang out. At any given time, Fuller's student body and faculty represent about 70 nations and approximately 120 denominations. Some of us come from Calvinist traditions, but we also have Wesleyans, Pentecostals, "new wave charismatics," Lutherans, Anglicans, and many others—including increasing numbers of Roman Catholics and Orthodox who have strong sympathies with evangelical Protestantism. And, of course, the cultural diversity makes for theological differences as well: a Korean Presbyterian is different from a Presbyterian from Nebraska, a Nigerian Anglican from his Australian Anglican counterpart, and so on.

Being exposed on a daily basis to the rich diversity of the body of Christ has taught me to look at more than the theology a person professes in judging his or her value to the kingdom of God. On this point I take encouragement from the way Charles Spurgeon defended John Wesley against the criticisms lodged by many of the Calvinists of Spurgeon's day. "While I detest many of the doctrines which he preached," wrote Spurgeon, "yet for the man himself I have a reverence second to no Wesleyan." He went on to comment as follows:

The character of John Wesley stands beyond all imputation for self-sacrifice, zeal, holiness, and communion with God; he lived far above the ordinary level of common Christians, and was one "of whom the world was not worthy." I believe there are multitudes of men who cannot see these [Calvinistic] truths, or, at least, cannot see them in the way in which we put them, who nevertheless have received Christ as their Savior, and are as dear to the heart of the God of grace as the soundest Calvinist in or out of Heaven.[55]

I am less inclined than Spurgeon to use a word like "detest" in describing my disagreement with many other evangelicals on important points of doctrine. But in this case I am glad he used that word, since it makes the contrast with his warm comments about Wesley's godliness even more impressive.

Spurgeon clearly believed that John Wesley loved the same gospel Calvinists love. In whatever way some of Wesley's theological formulations might have differed from those of Calvinist thought, there should be no doubt that he saw himself as a sinner who was totally dependent on sovereign grace for his salvation. I like Spurgeon's charitable spirit. Rather than insisting that only Calvinists are genuine Christians, I prefer to think that Calvinism best captures experiences and concerns that are at work in the lives of everyone who knows what it's like to plead for divine mercy out of a recognition of our own unworthiness.

Doctrine is very important. But it is not everything. Like Spurgeon, I stand in awe of the deep commitment to Christ I see in people whose professed theology often makes me quite nervous.

BEING OPEN TO CORRECTION

But my openness to people whose theology is different from my own goes further than simply respecting them for their godly lives. I have also learned much from folks who do not share my Calvinist convictions. From them I have learned to see important *correctives* in other theological perspectives. For example, as a Calvinist I clearly want to place a strong emphasis on divine sovereignty. Indeed, we Calvinists are so single-minded in this that if we are ever faced with a choice between a theological formulation that diminishes God's sovereignty and one that would diminish human freedom, we'll go with sovereignty. We would rather err on the side of underemphasizing human responsibility than to detract in any way from the sovereign rule of God over all things.

Most other theological perspectives place a greater emphasis on human freedom. In doing so, they often give the impression that God is limited by our human choices. Needless to say, this sort of thing makes me nervous. But I also see tendencies in my own Calvinism that make me nervous. Christians who specialize in free-will-centered theologies, for example, typically do a much better job at evangelism than Calvinists do. I believe that evangelism is extremely important. Rather than simply railing away at the alleged errors of those other theologies, then, I find it most helpful to look at the correctives they are supplying for Calvinists like me.

GETTING A SECOND OPINION

The other category of lessons I learned has to do with what I see as the need to recognize a variety of theological *specializations*. I find it helpful to see some of the theological differences that exist in the Christian community as stemming from something like the different specialized areas of expertise we see in the medical profession. Some physicians focus primarily on preventative medicine, others on correcting existing problems. Some incline toward surgical solutions, while others generally prefer noninvasive strategies.

In the big picture, all of these medical specializations have their place. This is why it's always important to consider getting a second opinion when dealing with a medical problem. And in weighing conflicting professional recommendations, it is necessary to take the specializations of the recommenders into account.

The world of theology also has its specializations. This was brought home in a very practical way during my student days when I had a teacher who was a committed Christian pacifist. I was very fond of him as a teacher, but I did not agree with his pacifist views and I would often stay after class to argue with him. He was a gentle man, and he patiently dealt with my objections to his views. One day I rather passionately threw out a challenge that pacifists are accustomed to hearing. "Suppose the Communists came to your home," I asked, "and threatened to kill you and your whole family, and suppose you had a chance to stop them by using violence—wouldn't you forsake your pacifist principles in that kind of situation?" He replied by saying that even then he would not use violence. "Why not?" I asked. "Because killing us is not the worst thing they could do to me and my loved ones," he answered. "Well, what *is* the worst thing?" I shot back. I have never forgotten his response: "The worst thing any human being could do to me and my family is to separate us from the love of Jesus. But I know that no human being can really do that." And then he quoted from memory the wonderful passage from Romans 8:

> For I am persuaded, that neither death, nor life, nor angels, nor principalities, nor powers, nor things present, nor things to come, nor height, nor depth, nor any other creature, shall be able to separate us from the love of God, which is in Christ Jesus our Lord.
> *Romans 8:38–39 KJV*

I never became the pacifist he would have liked me to be. But I've never forgotten the lesson he taught me. My own willingness to endorse the use of violence in many real-life situations is, as I see it, correct. But it is also dangerous. I risk the danger—and my pattern of questioning to him was evidence of this—that I will lean toward putting my ultimate trust in violent means of protection. His answer reminded me of something I was not inclined to be sensitive to in dealing with the hypothetical case I was presenting, namely, that our only real safety must be found in God, and that the worst thing that can happen to a human being is to be cut off from this source of safety. My teacher saw this more clearly than I did because he *specialized* in thinking about matters of ultimate "defense."

When I encounter what looks like a deep theological difference, I try to remind myself to ask what specialization might be at work in the other person's way of viewing things, and how I might learn from it. I realize that many other Christians—including probably most Calvinists—will find this to be a rather messy way of dealing with theological differences. But I have also learned to allow for a certain degree of messiness in my theology.

PUZZLES AND MYSTERIES

I like the description of the theological task given by a British monk named Thomas Weinandy. He says we should not think of theology primarily as a problem-solving activity. Rather, it is best understood as "a mystery-discerning enterprise." When we solve a problem, all of our puzzles disappear, and this is not what we should normally expect in theological exploration. The most we can usually hope for when we think carefully about a theological topic, he says, is to see "more precisely and clearly what the mystery is."[56]

This seems right to me. While I love the TULIP doctrines, I know they don't make many puzzles go away. But they do help me discern the mysteries of how a sovereign God draws rebel sinners to himself, restoring them to the purposes for which they were originally created. I try to keep a primary focus on that set of mysteries. But I have to realize that I also need a lot of theological help from Christians who have cultivated some rather different theological specializations.

chapter 12

KEEPERS OF THE MEMORIES

began this book by talking about a movie that poked some fun at Calvinism. I'll now end my discussion with a reference to another movie, this one based on a science fiction novel—*Fahrenheit 451*—by Ray Bradbury. The novel is a classic of sorts, but I find the movie, which has the same title, more gripping, especially in its final scene.

The story takes place in a future totalitarian society where it is forbidden to read books. In that society, the fire department doesn't put out fires; it *starts* them! Whenever a secret cache of books is discovered, the fire department is called to go and burn the books. Ray Bradbury took his title from the temperature—451 degrees Fahrenheit—at which paper bursts spontaneously into flame.

BECOMING A LOVER OF BOOKS

At the beginning of the story, the hero is a member of the fire department. But on one book-burning assignment he surprises himself by pocketing one of the books. Later he reads it in secret, and, to make a long story short, he becomes a lover of books. Soon he makes contact with a secret network of book preservers. When his activities are exposed to the authorities, he escapes to a remote colony of people who have banded together to keep the memories of books alive.

At the end of the book, he is being given a tour of this colony—which will be his new home—where each member has been assigned a book whose contents they are memorizing. The people in this colony live in the hope that the day will come when books are permitted again. When that happens, they want to be sure there are people alive who have preserved the memories of great books so that the contents can once again be returned to the printed page.

The first woman the hero encounters on his tour greets him with these words: "Hello, I am Plato's *Republic*." Then his guide points out other individuals, all of whom walk around and speak the contents of the books they have memorized. "That woman there," he says, "she is Emily Bronte's *Wuthering Heights*." The guide points to another man who is *Alice in Wonderland* by Lewis Carroll. Still another person is *Pilgrim's Progress* by John Bunyan. And on it goes—including a moving scene where an old man lying in a bed dies just after hearing his grandson finish reciting from memory the book whose contents the grandfather had passed on to the young boy.

TAKING THE CALVINIST VOW

That story serves as a parable of sorts for me. It represents something of our present theological situation. To be sure, the picture is much too stark—too apocalyptic—to be taken literally. But in certain ways it captures the mood of our time.

Of course, no one today is trying to burn the older books of theology. In the society in which I live at least, there are no laws against being a Calvinist. But I do find the Las Vegas airport scene to be a poignant one. For all of his theological ineptness, the George C. Scott character is trying to maintain something that is totally out of step with the people around him. Niki is only an extreme example of a more general kind of spiritual and theological cluelessness about what it is that is at work in Jake's life. Jake really belongs to a remote colony in which people are working at remembering things that the rest of the world is eager to forget.

When I first joined the faculty at Calvin College, I had an important conversation with Stanley Wiersma, a veteran English professor. I had just finished my doctoral work at the University of Chicago, and Stanley wanted to talk to me about the transition from a large secular university to a campus where people insisted that you subscribe to the old Calvinist teachings. "Coming here," Stanley said to me, "is a lot like joining a monastic order. In deciding to become a monk, a person leaves behind most of the values of the contemporary world, and he takes a vow to adopt a way of life that most people in the world have long forgotten. That's what we Calvinists here are like. We have taken a vow to do our teaching and our scholarship in ways that are different from the ways in which our universities trained us."

That image had a big influence on the way I understood my role as a professor at Calvin College. Over the years, though, I have taken Stanley's advice to an even deeper level. It isn't just being a Calvinist teacher-scholar that is a vow-taking kind of thing. It is at the heart of what it means for me to be a Calvinist as such. Benjamin Warfield showed the same sort of charitable spirit that Spurgeon had shown toward John Wesley when Warfield wrote in 1904 that all true Christians, whatever their theology, are Calvinists when they pray—when Christians are praying, he said, they speak "as if they were dependent on God's mercy alone." The person who has been convinced of Calvinism, however, said Warfield, "is determined to preserve the attitude he takes in prayer in all his thinking, in all his feeling, and in all his doing." All true Christians, Warfield remarked, "are Calvinists on their knees." What makes some people into consistent Calvinists, said Warfield, is the decision that in everything they do, with their minds, their hearts, and their bodies, they "shall remain on their knees continually, and only from this attitude think, feel, and act."[57]

To be a Calvinist is to make a special vow to work at that kind of consistency. We pledge to honor God's sovereignty, not only on our knees, but in all that we think and feel and do—while also insisting that we will make explicit reference to this in our theological formulations. To take this vow today, however, is to do so in an environment that is much more out of step, not only with the larger culture, but even with the larger Christian community. When Jonathan Edwards complained in the eighteenth century that the term *Calvinist* was a matter "of reproach," he did not know how good he had it in comparison to what would happen in later centuries. When people criticized Calvinism in his day, they at least had some idea of what they were talking about; their problem was that they simply did not like what Calvinism stood for. In most contemporary settings you would get more respect if you joined Niki in her "Venusian" convictions than you would if you announced that you considered yourself to be a Calvinist.

So this is where the contemporary Calvinist vow taking has some similarities to the plight of the *Fahrenheit 451* colony of book memorizers. For some of us at least, to be a Calvinist today also means that we will have to work at keeping alive the memories of older sayings and teachings in the hope that there will soon come a day when many others will want to learn such things again.

BELONGING TO THE COLONY

I'll tell you about my own personal version of this vow. I read and reread the Canons of Dordt. And in doing so, I have come to see myself as a member of a colony of memorizers.

The colony to which I belong cannot be found in an actual physical place. It is a network of Christians—each of us has made a vow to keep the memories of past theologies alive. Some of my fellow colonists are committed to Lutheran documents, others to the writings of John

Wesley or Anglicanism's Thirty-Nine Articles. Some of us are especially fond of catechisms, others of prayer books and the documents of ancient religious orders. We are an ecumenical lot—but our ecumenism makes much of the theological languages of the past. I am pleased to be a member of this colony. If someone should decide to make a *Fahrenheit 451*-type film of the colony, this is the one-liner I would like to speak: "Hi, I am the Canons of Dordt."

I do regularly read and reread the Canons. But that isn't all I do as a member of the colony. As I work alongside the other members, I see it as a part of my vow to remind them constantly of the Calvinist perspective and of what it means to explore important matters of faith from that particular way of viewing things. I talk a lot about our shared depravity and our total reliance on God's sovereign grace. And when the opportunity comes my way, I also feel compelled to proclaim in Kuyperian tones—although only after I have taken my daily dose of spiritual Prozac!—that Christ is the sovereign Lord and King over every square inch of creation.

But I also think a lot about Jake's awkwardness in the Las Vegas airport. And I think about the Nikis who are so much a part of the world in which I live. And I keep reminding myself that Calvinism at its best—both the "mere" and the "more"—is nothing but an elaborate way of explaining what my grandmother and her kind memorized from the Heidelberger in the spiritual colony they inhabited: My "only comfort in life and death" is "that I with body and soul, both in life and death, am not my own, but belong unto my faithful Savior Jesus Christ; who, with his precious blood, hath fully satisfied for all my sins, and delivered me from all the power of the devil."

That still travels well.

NOTES

1. John Calvin, *Institutes of the Christian Religion,* ed. John T. McNeill, trans. Ford Lewis Battles (Philadelphia: Westminster, 1960).
2. A standard work of this sort is Louis Berkhof, *Systematic Theology* (Grand Rapids: Eerdmans, 1949).
3. Jonathan Edwards, *Freedom of the Will,* Works of Jonathan Edwards, ed. Paul Ramsey (New Haven, Conn.: Yale Univ. Press, 1957), 131.
4. See Richard Mouw, *The Smell of Sawdust: What Evangelicals Can Learn from Their Fundamentalist Heritage* (Grand Rapids: Zondervan, 2000).
5. All of these can be found in Philip Schaff, ed., *The Creeds of Christendom, with a History and Critical Notes,* vol. 3 (Grand Rapids: Baker, 1996); they can be viewed on the Web at www.crcna.org/cr/crbe/index.htm.
6. Spurgeon's "Election" sermon can be found at www.spurgeon.org/sermons/0041.htm. The published copy I first read was in *Spurgeon's Sermons,* vol. 2 (Grand Rapids: Zondervan, n.d.), 66–87.
7. Charles Spurgeon, "A Defense of Calvinism"; can be viewed on the Web at www .spurgeon.org/calvinis.htm.
8. Ibid.
9. Ibid.
10. Ibid.
11. Peter De Vries, *The Mackerel Plaza* (New York: Penguin, 1986), 32.
12. Heidelberg Catechism, Question and Answer 8, emphasis added.
13. Canons of Dordt, Third and Fourth Main Points of Doctrine, Article 3.
14. Spurgeon, "A Defense of Calvinism."
15. Charles A. Howe, *The Larger Faith: A Short History of American Universalism* (Boston: Skinner House Books, 1993), 5. This understanding of Universalism as an expanded version of Calvinism is developed at some length by Ann Lee Bressler, *The Universalist Movement in America, 1770–1880* (New York: Oxford Univ. Press, 2001), in her first chapter titled "Calvinism Improved," 9–30.
16. Francis Thompson, "The Hound of Heaven"; can be viewed on the Web at http://poetry.elcore.net/HoundOfHeavenInRtT.html.
17. Owen Thomas, *The Atonement Controversy in Welsh Theological Literature and Debate, 1707–1841,* trans. John Aaron (Edinburgh: Banner of Truth, 2001), xix.
18. Ibid., 287.

19. Ibid., 132.

20. Ibid., 341.

21. Ibid.

22. Spurgeon's differences with his "hyper-Calvinist" critics are laid out nicely by Iain H. Murray in *Spurgeon v. Hyper-Calvinism: The Battle for Gospel Preaching* (Edinburgh: Banner of Truth, 1995).

23. Quoted in Murray, *Spurgeon v. Hyper-Calvinism*, 76.

24. Herman Hoeksema, "Jesus Savior and the Evil of Hawking Him"; can be viewed on the Web at www.rsglh.org/jesus_savior_and_the_evil_of_hawking.him.htm.

25. Spurgeon, "A Defense of Calvinism."

26. David J. Wolpe, *The Healer of Shattered Hearts: A Jewish View of God* (New York: Penguin, 1990), 140.

27. Ibid., 141.

28. Ibid.

29. Ibid., 158.

30. H. M. Kuitert, *I Have My Doubts: How to Become a Christian Without Being a Fundamentalist* (Valley Forge, Pa.: Trinity Press International, 1993), 97.

31. Wolpe, *The Healer of Shattered Hearts*, 159.

32. C. S. Lewis, *A Grief Observed* (New York: Seabury, 1961), 54–55.

33. Jerry Sittser, *A Grace Disguised: How the Soul Grows Through Loss* (Grand Rapids: Zondervan, 1995), 135–36.

34. Ibid., 142–43.

35. Ibid., 143.

36. See J. D. Douglas, *Light in the North: The Story of the Scottish Covenanters* (Grand Rapids: Eerdmans, 1964), 13.

37. Frank E. Gaebelein, *The Christian, The Arts, and Truth: Regaining the Vision of Greatness* (Portland, Ore.: Multnomah, 1985), 154–55.

38. Abraham Kuyper, *Lectures on Calvinism* (Grand Rapids: Eerdmans, 1931).

39. Kuyper's influence on evangelical intellectuals in North America has been highlighted in two major discussions of the recent emergence of a vital evangelical scholarship: one in the Roman Catholic magazine *Commonweal,* James C. Turner, "Something to Be Reckoned With: The Evangelical Mind Awakens" (www.commonwealmagazine.org/1999/990115/990115ar.htm), and the other in an *Atlantic* cover story, Alan Wolfe, "The Opening of the Evangelical Mind" (www.theatlantic.com/issues/2000/10/wolfe.htm).

40. Quoted in Louis Praamsma, *Let Christ Be King: Reflections on the Life and Times of Abraham Kuyper* (Jordan Station, Ontario: Paideia, 1985), 49.

41. Abraham Kuyper, *To Be Near Unto God,* trans. John Hendrik De Vries (Grand Rapids: Baker, 1925).

42. Abraham Kuyper, "Sphere Sovereignty," in *Abraham Kuyper: A Centennial Reader,* ed. James D. Bratt (Grand Rapids: Eerdmans, 1998), 488.

43. Dave Hunt, *What Love Is This? Calvinism's Misrepresentation of God* (Sisters, Ore.: Loyal Publishing, 2002).

44. For helpful comments on all of these few-versus-many passages, in support of the idea of divine generosity, see Neal Punt, *What's Good About the Good News? The Plan of Salvation in a New Light* (Chicago: Northland, 1988), 87–92.

45. Archibald Alexander Hodge, *Evangelical Theology: A Course of Popular Lectures* (Edinburgh: Banner of Truth, 1976), 401.

46. Westminster Confession of Faith, Chapter 10, "Of Effectual Calling," Articles 1 and 3; can be viewed on the Web at www.creeds.net/Westminster/wstmnstr.htm#chap10.

47. See my *Consulting the Faithful* (Grand Rapids: Eerdmans, 1994), 20–22.

48. Irvonwy Morgan, *Prince Charles's Puritan Chaplain* (London: Allen & Unwin, 1957), 162.

49. Quoted in Murray, *Spurgeon v. Hyper-Calvinism,* 94.

50. R. B. Kuiper, *As to Being Reformed* (Grand Rapids: Eerdmans, 1926), 88. The Warfield comment is from Benjamin Warfield, "What Is Calvinism?" in *Benjamin B. Warfield: Selected Shorter Writings,* vol. 1, ed. John E. Meeter (Phillipsburg, NJ: Presbyterian & Reformed Publishing, 1970), 389.

51. Kuiper, *As to Being Reformed,* 86.

52. Ibid., 92.

53. See Karl Rahner, "Anonymous Christians," in *Theological Investigations,* vol. 6 (Baltimore, Md.: Helicon, 1969), 390–98.

54. Calvin, *Institutes of the Christian Religion,* 2.2.11, 268–69.

55. Spurgeon, "A Defense of Calvinism."

56. Thomas G. Weinandy, O.F.M., Cap., *Does God Suffer?* (Notre Dame, Ind.: University of Notre Dame Press, 2000), 32–34.

57. Warfield, "What Is Calvinism?" 390.

INDEX

The Smell of Sawdust
What Evangelicals Can Learn from Their Fundamentalist Heritage
Richard J. Mouw

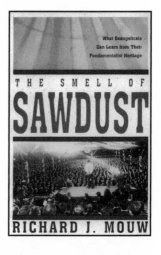

Richard Mouw's awareness of fundamentalism's problems hasn't robbed his appreciation for its strengths. *The Smell of Sawdust* sheds light on the colorful parentage of contemporary evangelicalism. If you detect fondness, even a hint of nostalgia, you're right. From its history to its mores and methods, Mouw takes you on a fascinating journey through the pros and cons of the "sawdust trail." Whatever your outlook on the revivalist tradition, these candid insights will inspire your respect for fundamentalism's strong points, help you learn from its weaknesses, and above all, enrich your life as a Christian. Like the author, you'll find yourself singing the old gospel hymns with new understanding.

The Smell of Sawdust is gentle and deeply personal. It is also wise—neither judgmental nor naive, but healing—furnishing redemptive insights into the character of our fundamentalist heritage. This book will broaden the perspective of thinking Christians who want to engage both their hearts and their intellects to reach the soul of our culture with the gospel.

Hardcover: 0-310-23196-5

Pick up a copy today at your favorite bookstore!

GRAND RAPIDS, MICHIGAN 49530 USA

WWW.ZONDERVAN.COM

ABOUT THE AUTHOR

Richard J. Mouw (Ph.D., University of Chicago) joined the faculty of Fuller Theological Seminary as professor of Christian philosophy in September 1985, after seventeen years as a professor at Calvin College in Grand Rapids, Michigan. He served for four years as provost and senior vice president under then-president David Hubbard, and in 1993 he was inaugurated as the fourth president of Fuller Theological Seminary, one of the largest seminaries in North America. Dr. Mouw has served Fuller as teacher, scholar, administrator, and public interpreter of evangelicalism.

Dr. Mouw has written many books and has also authored articles, reviews, and essays appearing in more than thirty journals. Among his books are *The God Who Commands: A Study in Divine Ethics; Uncommon Decency: Christian Civility in an Uncivil World; Consulting the Faithful; He Shines in All That's Fair: Culture and Common Grace; Wonderful Words of Life: Hymns in American Protestant History and Theology;* and *The Smell of Sawdust: What Evangelicals Can Learn from Their Fundamentalist Heritage.* Dr. Mouw is a regular columnist for the "Beliefnet" Web magazine (www.beliefnet.com).

We want to hear from you. Please send your comments about this book to us in care of zreview@zondervan.com. Thank you.

GRAND RAPIDS, MICHIGAN 49530 USA

WWW.ZONDERVAN.COM